MW01487816

WHAT COMES NEXT

Voyaging the Bible

TREVOR WAYNE ROLLS JR.

WESTBOW
PRESS®
A DIVISION OF THOMAS NELSON
& ZONDERVAN

Cover photo by CayLee Warren.

This book is a work of non-fiction. Unless otherwise noted, the author and the publisher make no explicit guarantees as to the accuracy of the information contained in this book and in some cases, names of people and places have been altered to protect their privacy.

WestBow Press books may be ordered through booksellers or by contacting:

WestBow Press
A Division of Thomas Nelson & Zondervan
1663 Liberty Drive
Bloomington, IN 47403
www.westbowpress.com
1 (866) 928-1240

ISBN: 978-1-9736-5571-8 (sc)
ISBN: 978-1-9736-5570-1 (hc)
ISBN: 978-1-9736-5572-5 (e)

Library of Congress Control Number: 2019902914

Print information available on the last page.

WestBow Press rev. date: 3/26/2019

To my wife, Jessica,
and my children, Daniel and Terah;
All my learning is in vain if I cannot share it with you.
I love you all.

Acknowledgments and Thanks

It has certainly been an interesting journey writing and publishing this book. I feel compelled to first acknowledge and thank God. Much prayer went into this idea before I decided to go for it, and I, therefore, feel as though this is a unique calling and gift from God. Beyond that, my wife and my children are next to thank. My daughter for simply inspiring carefree joy in my heart, my son for being so interested in not only my work but mainly the word of God, and my wife for utterly supporting me in all that has gone into this project.

There are also several other people who played various roles. Thanks to my friend and long-time Bible teacher, Donald Zeoli Sr. for reading much of my manuscript and offering critiques along the way. Also thanks to my niece, CayLee Warren for providing the cover art. Finally, thanks to Pastor Neil Eaton of New Hope Chapel Plymouth for always encouraging me to go further and dig deeper in God's word.

There are many others I would love to thank, but for sake of space I will conclude with thanking Regent University for offering me a solid education in biblical and theological studies, and finally, all the authors and professors who have given their lives to research, write, and teach the things I am simply repeating in my work. May God bless you all!

Foreword

Trevor Rolls and I have been married for almost seven years now, and I can honestly say that one of the most interesting and blessed parts of our marriage has been watching him come to know the Lord, and then growing in that relationship. Early on in his new-found faith in Jesus, Trevor strategized so he could get the most out of his studies, digging in and finding any useful information available to him in order that he might gain a deeper understanding of the Bible and what it teaches. Looking back now, though, I can see that it was so much more than simply his own strategy to get built up in the word of God, but that it was God building him up and preparing him for what would come.

It is important to know how to properly read and understand the Bible. In this book Trevor draws on his experience in finding out who he is in Christ, his work in preparing Bible studies and sermons, and his ongoing education at Regent University to bring a clear and concise layout on how to navigate through the pages of the Bible. His attempt is to take much of the scholarly information he has encountered and make it easier and more presentable so that others might better understand. Having devoted his higher education to uncovering the truths about the Bible so he is fully equipped to answer questions people might have, Trevor also wants to be able to help people heal through the truth of knowing exactly what it means for Jesus to have died for our sins so we can be in right relationship with God. I once told Trevor how he reminds me of a superhero. He recoiled at first because he did not like me putting him on such a high pedestal, but I quickly explained that I thought this because he uses his "powers" of knowledge seeking to help people understand the Bible better and what it is trying to teach us, and that this leads people to salvation.

In the pages of his book, Trevor does just that by unpacking how we can read and understand the Bible, and why it is so important for us to do so. He makes it a point to cover many avenues in order to present the topic with precision and accuracy, but in the end he knows it is only the actual study of God's word that will bring you to a closer relationship with our Creator. I know he truly wants people to understand just how fully Jesus can and will impact their lives, and how blessed they will become once they develop that active and ongoing relationship with our wonderful Lord and savior through the study of his life-giving word.

Jessica Rolls

Contents

INTRODUCTION

Salvation in Christ is a glorious occasion. It is deliverance, new beginning, and redirection. It is also quite confusing. Of course, nobody wants to admit it. It is, however, true. This is why I write. I am currently groping my way through my sixth year as a Christian and third year of college, and all I feel like God is telling me to do, is stop holding back and go all in for the gospel. I mean, it's not as if I am doing nothing, I teach a study group, and I am a husband and father of two—add full-time college student with a side of work, and I suppose there is not a huge amount more I could be doing. Nevertheless, here we are.

I say all that because I wish to start our relationship off with honesty and introduction. I want you to know who I am. Of all the writers I read, I appreciate the most the ones who allow me to get to know them through their work. Not that this work is about me; it is actually about you, and your walk with Jesus, but I figure if you are anything like me, then I may as well provide you with what I would appreciate from an author.

I have, long since my salvation, come to believe that my writing is a spiritual gift. Most people want to tell me that it is my musical ability, but I have been playing music for over 20 years. Writing, on the other hand, is a new and exciting journey I make with God. I typically write academically, since I write most for my degree work. This usually means extensive research followed by what seems like endless amounts of footnotes to adequately cite all the sources that support my work. I am not so much doing that here. This book is for the everyday average Christian—the guy or gal who doesn't really care how many Phd's I cite in my bibliography, as long as I can help. That doesn't mean I won't use any outside sources, but it just means that I intend on trying to keep this as casual as possible. I truly hope that this book reads like an ongoing conversation you keep having with your favorite new friend at church.

That being said, I encourage you to investigate the sources I do use. These are valuable resources that can take you much deeper than my work will. Most of my sources are from my coursework in biblical and theological studies at Regent University. Some of the others are from my recreational readings, while yet others are books I heard about from various pastors and preachers. So, even though it might seem tedious, check out the notes and see if you are interested in any of these works. Try to think about every work I reference as recommended reading for whatever topic they fall under. In the end, I am really not adding anything to these topics, but I believe each of us has a sphere of influence that somebody else may not have, and can, thus, reach people perhaps otherwise unavailable. For this reason, even if I am saying nothing new, it is important that I say it anyways. The simplest and purest motive in my heart is to, first, serve the Lord, and, second, help you. So, while I am definitely not claiming to be an expert in my field of study yet, I can certainly offer some tips and pieces advice about what you can expect, and what might be helpful for you.

I was fortunate in my first two years of being a Christian. I had a lot of people who encouraged me, prayed for me, mentored me, and genuinely just loved me. And God has done some wonderful things in my life, but even so, I still had tough times in those first years—as I do even now. I had questions, and I had concerns. I can only imagine how much more difficult it is for someone, then, who doesn't have the kind of support I had. So, this book is essentially made up of most of the basic things about the Bible and Bible study that I would want to share with somebody who I was taking under my wing as a disciple.

I can't say enough how much I pray this book helps and blesses you—and praise and glory be to God if it does because I know beyond any doubt that if anything here touches your heart, if anything here stretches or grows your faith, if anything here brings you further along in your Christian walk than you were before… then God is on the move. It is his doing, not mine. These are God's truths, not mine, so all the credit goes to him. On the other end, if there are any mistakes, if there are any offenses, if anything in this work comes across as low quality, inaccurate, unhelpful, or otherwise simply wrong or bad, then let it be my fault, not God's. He loves you.

CHAPTER 1

You've Taken the Plunge

The chapter title, I must confess, is somewhat borrowed. It is from one of the first chapters in a rather large volume on spiritual maturity, and it is basically saying, "You became a Christian. Great…Now what?"[1] I suppose I could just save us both the trouble and give you that book, but although I am launching from the same idea, I am not looking to give you a 500-page manual on spiritual maturity like Dr. Hanson. But we are looking to ask and answer the same question, "What should I do now?" So, however you found yourself here: maybe you were at a crusade or a conference, or maybe you gave your life to Christ at the end of a church service. Maybe you prayed with a preacher from the radio or television, or maybe you've been attending a little church somewhere and confessed Jesus as Lord. Whatever got you to this point, it is time to move forward.

Some people have a dramatic conversion experience where they feel instantly changed, while others have a progressive revelation where they slowly realize they have been welcomed into the kingdom of heaven. However it happened, or is happening for you, heaven is rejoicing all the same. Jesus says, "I tell you, there is joy in the presence of the angels of God over one sinner who repents (NASB)."[2] This is because of the great lengths God went through to provide you the means to be in his presence, and to have a relationship with him. How can we ever fully comprehend that this was set in motion since before the foundations of the earth were laid? How can we ever truly understand the work of Jesus Christ in his life, death, and resurrection for our atonement? How can we ever fully wrap our minds around the indwelling presence of the Holy Spirit? Yet, when we confessed Jesus as Lord, when we admitted our sins, asked for forgiveness, and turned to God in repentance, all of these things reached their culmination in our lives—in your life, and in mine.

I'm not sure where you are at right now, what kind of church you attend, or what denomination you belong to, but I am sure that if you did the things we just talked about, then, as Jesus said in Luke 15:10, heaven rejoices for the salvation of your soul. And I rejoice too! So let's talk about a few things concerning this strange new journey you are on.

There is No Thing Like the Church

If you really have committed to Christ, then your life will never be the same. If you're just kind of like sight-seeing—checking out the music, or maybe just trying to get points with that cute worship guy or pretty Christian chick, then you probably won't be around for long. Oh, it will be fun for a bit, but if your heart really isn't in it, when it gets hard—and it will get hard—you will quit. You also may think we can't tell...but we can, and even if we couldn't, God can. Honestly though, if that is you, stick around. You'll be surprised with what God can do with your doubts.

Now, for you who are a sold-out believer, there is no thing on earth like the Church. No, I'm not talking about the building you attend. The Church is you, and the Church is me. The Church

4

is the body of Christ, and it is moving in this world like never before! I say all this because I want you to realize that giving your life to Christ is unlike *anything* you have ever done. You are a member of the body of Christ, a soldier in the army of God, and a citizen in the kingdom of heaven. You are blood bought and redeemed, indwelt by the Holy Spirit, a new creation in Christ, and a representative of Christ to the world; you are, however, in many ways still you.

Because you are still you, mistakes will happen. God is sanctifying you, and he is rebuilding you from the inside out, but the process takes time—a lifetime to be exact. I can't tell you what kind of mistakes you will make, but I know you will make them because we all make them. You will mess up with a loved one. You will lash out at a co-worker. You will misunderstand what the Bible says. You will pass judgment on people. You will constantly wrestle with the you that once was and the you that now is. Ephesians 4:22-24 says,

> In reference to your former manner of life, you lay aside the old self, which is being corrupted in accordance with the lusts of deceit, and that you be renewed in the spirit of your mind, and put on the new self, which in the likeness of God has been created in righteousness and holiness of the truth (NASB).

The only problem is, that old self is still hanging right there in the closet. Sure, it will probably be a while before you give it a second thought, but soon enough the devil comes calling. Maybe it is a couple months, maybe a couple years, but eventually you'll try it on again. Oh, maybe not the whole outfit. Maybe just the pants or the shirt. Maybe just the socks. These are the mistakes we make, the things we do, but thank God that old self just doesn't fit anymore… even the socks.

Mistakes aren't always bad things either. There is always a new lesson to be learned from our mistakes, if we are willing to learn the lesson. That's why it is important to try and see the lesson through the mistake. You might say, "God, how could you let me do that?" It is much better though to say, "What can I learn from this?" It is a painful process, no doubt, but it is effective. I have been through it plenty in my struggle with lust and pornography. I say to God, "How could you let me end up here again? I thought you delivered me from this…" But then I have to examine myself, because I say, "Oh yeah, God *did* deliver me from this. So how did *I* end up here again?" And I have to examine my behavior. Looking at those Facebook posts I had no business looking at, or reading those whisper confessions that, although not pornographic, are not something a Christian after the heart of God should be entertaining himself with. And then it hits me, the voice of God inside my heart saying, "See what I'm trying to show you about yourself?"

It's a good process, but it is not something meant to be done alone. It is not even something meant to simply be between you and God. This is another reason why God gives us the Church, and it is another reason why the Church is a thing all of its own. When you get real with yourself, honest with yourself and honest with others, people will want to help you. Friends will be made— and not just those fair-weather types or the company of misery. You will make friends in the Church that will change your life, friends that will be there. You will gain friends in Christ that will hurt with you, pray with you, and walk through the fire with you. You will make friends who base their relationship with you on the goodness and glory of God, not on what you have to offer them, or not even you specifically. These are the friends you want, the friends that will walk with you through the trials of life, grow with you in Christ, and love you like only a brother or sister in the body Christ could.

Consequently, friends will also be lost. Because the Church is unlike anything else in the world, it will not go unnoticed by your current peer group. It's not like joining the Elks Lodge, or a book club. Jesus Christ will change your life, and though you will be loving the new you, your old buddies will not. They will see your change as threatening, and they will see it as convicting. They will accuse you, saying, "What, do you think you're better than us?" They will talk about you behind your back, sometimes slandering and spreading lies about you, and they will also criticize your faith to your face. They will hit you with all the hardest questions, they will lead you to compromising situations, and they will turn on you when they see you are not willing to compromise your faith or your integrity.

I know you probably do not believe me—not Kim, or not John. "I have known them for years." And true enough, not every person will outwardly express resentment for you, and there is the hope that some of your friends will even be inspired to follow Christ by the changes God causes in your life, but if you stick around long enough, you will see the truth in what I am saying about how coming to Christ often means leaving behind many of your old acquaintances. The funny thing is, the real kicker, the irony of it all, however, is that you will love them more now than you ever have in your life. You will love them with the love of Christ. The very Jesus they despise will be prompting you to love them with a love that could only come from God.

Some of the things I just mentioned probably sound a bit unpleasant. They are, after all, unpleasant situations to be in.

Nevertheless, if you are truly walking with Jesus. If this is it, you've made up your mind and there is nothing that can change it, then this will be the greatest adventure you have ever experienced. Even when the experience itself is not all you want or hope it to be (because sometimes it will not be), you can count on the fact that God is with you, and that you are a member on the body of Christ. There will be ups, and there will be downs, but God promises you this: "I will never desert you, nor will I ever forsake you (NASB)."[3]

What You Can Expect from Me

In the pages and chapters that follow, I will offer you some… *suggestions* that might help you on your journey. As I said before, I'm sure there are some things you might be confused about. Maybe you are embarrassed to ask about your confusions, or maybe you have asked and haven't gotten any good answers. Maybe you don't have anyone to ask, or maybe you just aren't the asking type. Or maybe none of this is the case, and you just want to see what this book has to say on the subject. Either way, what I am going to cover as we move forward should be regarded as helpful suggestions. I am not trying to tell you what to do, but I am not going to caution the phrasing of every statement I make and, thus, waste both of our time. If I say you should do something, then I really think you should, but that doesn't mean the curtain is closed on that issue and there is no room for variation. God is never changing, but we are all so different that he often deals with us all in somewhat different ways.

That being said, God is very consistent. He is solid as a rock, a firm foundation, and a mighty fortress. So, in that sense, there are things that will never change about his dealings with you. Your sin, for instance, will *always* be offensive to him. You will always need to confess and repent. You will always do better when you are walking closely with him, and you will always have hardships and failures when you play fast and loose with his commands and his ways. You will find this out because you will test this at times, and praise Jesus that he is faithful and patient to work with us through our stumbling because you will stumble—we all do.

I cannot offer you a detailed walk through your Christian journey—nobody really can, although some claim to be able to. We have, however, come back around to the point of this chapter and really of this whole book: what comes next... You've taken the plunge, you are now a Christian, so here is what you should do now. As Dr. Hanson mentions in his work, most of us are encouraged by others or led by our own understanding to jump right into service. He goes on to say, and I am inclined to agree, that "God is concerned more about your life than He is your service!"[4] This basically means that God is more concerned with your walk with him, with developing and growing you, and with creating a testimony in you, than he is with you setting up chairs or playing guitar with the worship team.

If you think about it, this really makes sense. When you serve God in a church, you also represent God and the Church to anyone you encounter. If you are not right in the heart, you can end up making a mess of things. Not to mention, God loves *you*, and he wants to develop you. If you jump right into service, you won't get that time of growth and change in him that you really need. God can find anyone to be an usher or teach a study, and true enough, he will surely call on you someday to do a task he has prepared for you; don't sell yourself short in the meantime. Wait for that thing. Spend time growing and walking with Jesus, and when the time comes that he has some task he wants you to perform, when he has some mission he wants to send you on—even if the mission is something that seems simple and menial like parking cars or setting up chairs—he will let you know when he wants you to do it.

Walking with Jesus should be a simple concept, one would think, but for whatever reason, it seems to have become harder and harder an idea to grasp. Perhaps it is because of our aversion to change, or maybe it's that ingrained American attitude that nobody tells me what to do. Perhaps it is media or perhaps it's culture; whatever *it* is, it is apparent that walking with Jesus is not spelled out as loudly and clearly in this present day and age than it has been in the past. When we join the church, the most common thing we think is, "what can I do?" Doing stuff, however, is not the answer to any of our problems. I know it may seem counterintuitive, but if we want real, measurable growth, then we need to be willing to unhook from whatever plow each of us may be yoked to and tie ourselves up to Jesus instead; we need to be willing to step back in our walk of life and say, "Jesus, why don't you take lead. I'll follow."

What many of us do, however, looks quite different. The preacher calls for change, and the congregation cries legalism. The Bible speaks of sin, and culture calls that oppression. We want to make our own choices. We want to lead our own lives, but the fact of the matter is that we are never really blazing the trail. We, one way or another, end up following something or someone. Most of the time, if it isn't Jesus then it is culture because culture collectively seeks cosmetic comfort. Even church culture can be unhealthy for a person who hasn't truly developed their relationship with Jesus because we are all so busy doing stuff, that a person can get caught up into all that stuff doing, and never realize that the stuff we do is a byproduct of our relationship with God, not a path to establishing and maintaining that relationship.

When we miss this, we can end up being exactly like the works-driven cultures of the world.

True Christianity, however, is countercultural—Jesus is countercultural! And while growth with Christ is far from oppressive, it can be uncomfortable at times. Jesus, after all, has a habit of making people uncomfortable with their sin. None of this is bad, although it may be different than what you have heard, and it is certainly different from the ways of the world which seek to cover up our shortcomings by exploiting our strengths in a sort of sleight of hand maneuver that we might avoid the discomforts of growth and relax in whatever good works we can muster up. But if we were doing just fine the way we were, then would we ever have given our lives to Christ in the first place? For many of us, I suspect not. In that case, if any of us knew any better, we would embrace the change. Don't feel bad though, most of us do not—at least not while it is happening. We usually gripe, grope, and resist, but then enjoy the finished result to the glory of God.

But how do we get to a glorious finished project? We build on a firm foundation. The foundation of any venture is vastly important to its success. Think of space travel. With all the amazing technology involved with breaking free from the Earth's atmosphere and venturing into the open space of the universe, none of that would matter if not for the solid launch-pad from which the shuttle blasts off. It is the same with the Christian walk. We need a solid launch-pad to blast off from—a firm foundation to build on. I hope it is clear from the very beginning that I wish to build from no other place than the firm foundation of Jesus Christ, and for the purpose of bringing glory to his name. After all, nothing else really matters. Church growth, book success, preacher popularity, even personal growth, is all virtually worthless if it does not launch from the firm foundation of our wonderful Lord and Savior. All other ground, as the old hymn says, is shifting sand.

Conclusion

I labored to decide, when considering which aspects of the Christian experience to teach, whether to first discus prayer, or whether it should be Bible study. They are both very important, but since developing a prayer life is such a hard thing to nail down, and since it is actually the Bible that teaches us to pray, I decided to start with Bible study. I don't want to offer too much here on that, so as not to be repeating myself when the chapters are read, but simply stated, you need Bible study or else you are literally taking other broken people's word on how you should live, what you believe, and what you have waiting for you on the other side. I will tell you about various ways to study the Bible, such as studying its contents or studying its historical reliability. I will also address some of the slanders and accusations against the Bible which I am sure you have heard. Other topics discussed will include the belief of biblical inspiration and the topic of Bible translations. Finally, I will give you tips on exactly how to study the texts, interpret what it says, and how to apply it to your life.

As I said before, I hope that this book acts as a sort of ongoing conversation, and I hope that I can adequately offer you insight on some of the questions that often come up in the first phases of a person's walk with Christ. Honestly, I hope you don't even need my book. It would be better for you to have honest and capable Bible teachers in your life. But even if you do, this could be a helpful conversation starter with them so you can get real face to face instruction. I don't want to come across like a person who thinks they have all the answers either. I challenge you to test every single thing I teach against the Bible. I, after all, am not infallible and inerrant; that honor belongs to God and his word. So, again, test me, challenge me, question me, ask your pastors and elders about the things I say, and search the Scriptures to see if the things I am teaching are correct. If you do that, then I am doing my job, and God is glorified.

So, now that you know what to expect, I hope that you are as eager as I am to jump into these chapters. I pray this book helps you and strengthens you on your journey with Jesus, and if you are not a Christian yet, I pray this book can lead you to an encounter with the real and true risen and living Jesus. All that being said, now that you've taken the plunge, let's go for a swim together in the pages of God's word.

CHAPTER 2

Swimming in the Word of God

I am convinced that nobody ever really knows what the Bible is when they first start reading it. Not to mention that, but given the cultural gap and difference of a couple thousand years, I think most people just don't know what to do with it. I mean, I think most are aware we are supposed to read it, but when it actually comes down to the task, like dipping one's foot in a cold pond, we often resist the uncomfortable water. But the words in the Bible are not like some murky swamp, they are the refreshing pools and streams of living water. The Bible is cleansing to the soul, and it is like ointment and bandages for our damaged hearts and minds.

The Bible is very often and rightfully referred to as the word of God, and Jesus is also called the Word of God. The book of Ephesians says Jesus washes us with the waters of the word,[1] and in John 15:3, Jesus says he cleanses us with his word. This is why study is so important. When we dip our feet and want to resist, we should resist the urge to resist, and we should dive right in! Like a cool and clear pool on a hot day, how awesome and refreshing is it to dive in the deep end and actually swim? Sure, I know some like to slowly enter the shallows, cringing at each step, hair slowly standing up as the cool water gets closer to the… more tender and hidden areas. How many times though, do these people abort and exit the water? But when you dive in, you are all at once submersed, shocked and refreshed, and with no turning back. You are stimulated to move around, to swim, and to explore.

You feel alive when you are in the water, and the more often you swim, the better you feel. You become strong, toned and conditioned, and you build up stamina and endurance—but you have to keep coming back. You have to keep returning to the pool. You have to keep diving in, and you have to keep swimming. This is how it is with the Bible. It's not always easy to do, just as it is not always easy to keep consistent on your laps. Some days you don't want to, and even when you manage, you want to quit before you even work up a sweat. This is when you have to press in. This is where you decide how close you really want your walk with Jesus to be.

You have to want the results more than you don't want to do the work—any personal trainer will tell you this, and training in the Bible is no different. The time you spend in Bible study will make or break your Christian development. There's just no way around it. Coupled with prayer, your Bible study habits will ultimately decide whether you have a close walk with the Lord... or if you do not.

Reading Versus Study

If you want growth, if you want to know God, and if you want direction in your Christian walk, then you have to read *and* study the Bible. I would also add, that if your church or group, or denomination or mentors, or anyone else discourages you from reading the Bible—or if they insist that you can only truly understand it by their enlightenment or with their additional resources—something is amiss and you should seek alternative fellowship. I'm not saying there won't be questions you need to ask someone who has been studying longer than you have, but you need to be reading your Bible—and I'm not just talking about on Sunday at church either.

Personal growth requires a personal walk with God and time in personal reading, prayer, and study…And no truly Christian person or group would ever discourage you from this. Many call it devotional time, and rightfully so; it takes devotion to really set aside time for God. Church is good, fellowship is good, Christian entertainment and worship music are good, and they all have their place, but it is quality time spent studying the word of God that will really stretch and grow your understanding of what you are doing in your faith, or of what any of it even means.

An example of this in my own life has do with a specific song, "Hosanna,"[2] and then my first Palm Sunday as a Christian. As I mentioned in the introduction, I am a musician. I play multiple instruments, and I love to write and record songs. So, music really stands out to me. I speak the language. But this song, "Hosanna," really bothered me. I mean, it had good parts and a nice flow, but something about it really just got to me. It was the name, which is also the main cry of the chorus, "Hosanna, Hosanna, Hosanna in the highest."[3] I didn't get it, so it really bugged me.

Well, fast forward a few months to my first Christian Easter celebration (actually, it was the Sunday before Easter). There it was, everywhere—Hosanna city. I'm like, "What is it with this crazy word that sounds so weird, and that everybody keeps saying?" I did some asking around, and I learned it was a phrase from the Bible, and that it had to do with Jesus entering Jerusalem just prior to his crucifixion. From there, I hit the books and learned that the term Hosanna held prophetic connotations from the Old Testament,[4] and that when the crowds were shouting Hosanna at

Jesus when he entered Jerusalem in the New Testament,[5] they were actually acknowledging him as the Messiah. So, because of one *word study*, I was able to both enjoy the song and fully appreciate the Palm Sunday celebration.

That was just one kind of study. There are other types of study, as well as simply reading. Studying in different ways has different benefits. Also, reading has its own benefits. It is important to note, however, that reading and studying are different. I know this probably sounds like it is complicated, but it really is not. Let's break it up a bit, and try to make some sense out of what I am saying here.

Reading

Reading is exactly what it sounds like. This is a time when you simply read through the material. I tend to do this during my morning devotional time. I'm not trying to intentionally learn something, I'm not trying to gain any profound theological insight, and I'm really not even trying to memorize anything. I am simply reading the words off the page. I pick a book of the Bible, and I read through it. Sometimes I'll read a chapter or two in a sitting, and other times ill read multiple chapters. Sometimes I even read whole books. It really depends on how much time I have, and on what book I am reading. If I'm reading one of Paul's letters, then I may take four or five chapters in one sitting. Depending on the letter, I might even read the whole thing. Some of them are pretty short. On the other hand, if I'm reading through one of the Gospels, then I will probably only get two or three chapters down in a normal sitting. I try not to jump around though. I have found it best, at the suggestion of many authors and teachers, to pick a book and stick with it till it is complete—this helps you get the whole message that was intended. I also like to backtrack a couple paragraphs or a chapter when I read—especially if a day or two has gone by since my last reading. This way, I get refreshed on what the author was thinking, and I can pick back up on the flow of the writing.

So, if I'm not trying to learn anything during my reading, then why am I doing it? Well, I want to lend my ear to God. I want to give him that time to speak to me if he wants to. I want to become familiar with what these books are saying. Familiarity is so important, but it is also often taken for granted. One of my professors thought so highly of becoming familiar with the material that he wanted us to read Philippians 40 times before beginning our final project. He knew that this is how you begin to build up a basic knowledge of the Bible, and he wanted to instill that in us. But the idea goes so much beyond simply gathering knowledge, this is also where you start to really figure out what you think of it all. This is where you develop questions and curiosities, and it is when you make connections. During these reading times, God causes things to jump up off the pages at you. Certain sentences, words, phrases, or even whole concepts will come alive in your mind and heart. Then, the next thing you know, you have some things you want to actually study. You have questions you want answered. You have verses you want explained, and you have legitimate, specific, and personal reasons to want to dig deeper.

All of that being said, it is a good idea to keep a pad and a pen nearby. This is something one of my mentors taught me and swears by. Like I said, your reading time should be just that, simply reading. But also like I said, questions and curiosities will arise. You don't want to have to stop your reading to go investigate these questions and curiosities, but also you don't want to forget them. Your personal desire to understand things will take you so much further at times than pre-packaged lessons presented to you in a sermon or some other teaching. So make notes of these things as you read, that way you can follow up on them later. Doing this in our reading times often provides material to take into our study times. This is another reason why it is so important to have both (reading and study).

Having said that, let's take a look at the study aspect of things. But before we do, I would like to just add that I'm not saying you have to read the Gospel of John 40 times to understand it (I was working on a specific assignment where we were to create a four or eight part lesson plan for the book of Philippians, that's why he wanted us to read it so many times), but there certainly is a high value to reading passages numerous times to get familiar with them before you start cracking open commentaries to get other people's opinions on them (It also helps you be able to follow along with the commentary...more on that later). Now, let's take a look at some different study tools.

Bible Study and Study Bibles

There are so many approaches to studying that it is hard to imagine listing them all here, but we can get the basic concepts, motivations, and ideas. Like I said, study comes from a desire to know more, and a desire to know more comes largely from reading the Bible. Apart from there being several ways to study, there are also a number of tools available such as Bible concordances, Bible dictionaries, and Bible commentaries. Another very popular tool in Bible study is what we call the *Study Bible*.

The study Bible is different from the cheaper Bibles, or the free ones you receive from a church or find in a hotel room drawer (Do they still do that?). Study Bibles often contain notes, articles, and even customized study plans. Many of them have a brief introduction to each book that lets you know what's going on—who is writing, when it was written, why they wrote it, and so on. On top of this, footnotes often accompany the texts to explain things we might miss due to cultural differences or things like that. Because of these things, I would say that anyone who is serious about wanting to study the Bible *needs* to get a good study Bible. I actually have several because they come in so many different disciplines. For instance, one Bible I have is *The Archaeological Study Bible*.[6] This Bible consistently presents various articles on archaeological findings relevant to the different verses, chapters, and books as you read through them. All of the footnotes are also specifically geared towards archaeology. Another one is the *Thompson Chain-Reference Study Bible*.[7] This Bible has a number-coded mapping system so you can find related topics to the verse you are reading. You can also get study Bibles with the commentary written by famous preachers—this way you can get their take and their explanations as you read.

I don't say all this to show off how many study Bibles I have. My Bibles don't really do *you* any good, but I want you to be aware that these resources are out there and what they are useful for. Now, don't get me wrong, the world has been walking with Jesus for hundreds of years without topical study Bibles. However, that doesn't mean they aren't useful. When I get to know a person, what their situation is, what their struggles are, and the needs they have, I am able to find a Bible with helpful insights geared toward them. Bibles geared towards the struggles of men, Bibles geared towards addiction recovery, Bibles for women, for teens, and for pastors are all useful tools for helping a person grow in Christ. The Bible is for everyone, but chances are there is a study Bible specifically for you.

Word Studies and a Concordance

I mentioned a *word study* earlier. In the word study, you pick a word…and you study it (I know, profound, right?). I chose the word Hosanna, but people do word studies on all sorts of words from Christ, to Spirit, to synagogue, to faith, to you name it. Basically, you pick a word and look it up in a concordance, and the concordance tells you every place that word is found in the Bible. From here, you look up all the different verses so you can get a general idea of what the biblical context of that word is. A word of caution is in order however. Word studies are a great way to get your feet wet at understanding certain words in different contexts, but because word studies show you the chosen word in many different contexts, it can be easy to get confused or mixed up if you are placing too much doctrinal emphasis on a simple word study. Things like the Rapture, the Second Coming, Heaven and Hell, these things are by no means immune to the benefit of word studies, but for a deep and adequate understanding you often need to go deeper into context than what a word study typically offers. That's alright though. Bible study is all about going deeper at your own pace—just like swimming in water, as I mentioned earlier.

The main tool for word studies would be what we call a concordance. A very popular one is *Strong's Exhaustive Concordance of the Bible*.[8] This is a good tool because it is a massive map of sorts. It tells you where to go to find the word you want to study. Also, many of these books also have the Greek or Hebrew word used in the original writing. I'll talk about this more in the later section on translation, but for now it should just be said that finding out the word's usage and context in the original language can sometimes add valuable insight to your study. The unfortunate thing about a concordance, however, is that for the most part, it sort of reads like a phone book (hopefully some of you remember what that is). In that sense, it is a very limited tool. Nevertheless, it definitely points you in the right direction for getting started in your study basic study of God's words.

Topical Studies and Bible Dictionaries

Branching out from a word study, you could do a topical study. No, not a *tropical* study, although that sounds nice. A topical study is kind of an extension of the word study, but instead of just a word, now you are studying a whole idea or, as the word topical implies, a specific topic. So, where a word study on faith would show you all the verses that say faith, a topical study on faith would seek to unpack those verses to really expand into the fundamental teachings on faith. Both the word study and the topical study could use the Bible concordance and Bible dictionary, and even a Bible Commentary. I think, however, that a Bible commentary is best suited for what we might call a verse by verse study. In the same sense, a dictionary is useful in the word study but it gives enough information to bring the reader well into the arena of what the topic is about over simply defining a word.

Pulling out a Bible dictionary for a topical study is much like pulling out a regular dictionary but also somewhat like consulting an encyclopedia. These books tend to go beyond a simple definition to offer explanations of what a word means in a biblical context. Considering that people study the Bible on many different levels, it should be noted that Bible dictionaries come from one end of the field to the other. That is to say that some of them are written very simply and geared toward the everyday average reader. Others are written with extreme detail and are geared towards academic and scholarly readers. These dictionaries are very useful tools, but if you are going to get one, it is important that you get one suited for your level of interest. A popular basic dictionary is the *Vine's Concise Dictionary*.[9] A more academic volume is the *New Dictionary of Theology*.[10] The importance of understanding the difference lies in the fact that a casual reader will be overwhelmed with an academic volume and an academic reader will be disappointed in a casual volume. When I read customer reviews on Amazon, the number one reason I come across for bad reviews is that the reader did not get what they needed—it was either too confusing or too simple. So again, make sure you get the right tool for the job because it is really hard to hammer in a nail with a screwdriver (but not impossible).

Verse by Verse Study and Bible Commentaries

In the verse by verse study, you go through a book, chapter, or passage one verse at a time, but unlike simply reading it, you take time and use study tools to gain a deep understanding of exactly what it means and how it ties in with the overarching message. In this type of study, you would check your commentary and also the footnotes in your study Bible to get an explanation of what each verse is saying. Now, I'm not saying there are hidden or secret meanings in the texts, but it is easy sometimes, because of cultural differences, to miss the *intended* meaning of a statement or passage—and that is why we study. The biggest benefit to verse by verse study is that you are getting a complete presentation of the author's work or thought. Many times, a person will quote a verse of Scripture to apply in a certain situation. However, when you go back and read that very profound sounding verse in its original context, sometimes you find out that it doesn't actually mean what you thought it meant. This is why it is important to read and study the Bible in larger chunks so you can make sure you are getting the intended message.

Using a Bible commentary is very helpful in verse by verse studies because the commentary author sort of narrates through the verses with an interpretive voice. Commentaries are typically written by people of higher education who, having done a lot of the proverbial leg-work, provide the reader with the results of many years of research and study. Often times commentaries will include much of the information provided by concordances and dictionaries with the main intent that the reader never loses sight of exactly what is going on in the passage. In short, the main job of a good commentary is to provide you with information and details about the verse, passage, or chapter while making sure to keep the reader anchored to the overall message and purpose of the whole writing.

Commentaries are great tools, but there are some things a person should make note of. Just like Bible dictionaries, commentaries are written from one end of the field to the other. There are very simple and selective Bible commentaries for casual readers, and there are very detailed and in depth works written for academic readers.[11] There are also one volume works and multiple volume sets. It is typically (but not always) the academic works that are broken up into multiple volumes, and is typically (but not always) the casual works that are condensed into one volume. In this case, just like the dictionaries, you want to make sure you are getting a commentary designed to offer what you are looking for. The best way to do this is to read online book reviews and see what the people who own a particular volume say about it. Also, since commentaries are typically written by a single person, one has to be aware that to some degree or the next you will be getting that particular person's interpretations, applications, and doctrinal preferences. This seems more common on the casual level than the academic level, but it is nevertheless a thing to be aware of on all levels.

Conclusion

Hopefully I have conveyed to you some helpful distinctions and tools for studying and reading the Bible. I know it can seem a bit overwhelming if you aren't familiar with any of this. And I'm not saying you should go out and immediately buy all the tools I mentioned. I would, however, suggest at least getting a good study Bible. I also really want to reinforce the importance of studying *and* reading the Bible. You need those times of just reading and taking it in, and you also need those times of really digging, pressing, searching, and scrutinizing. These will both grow your understanding, and also your faith. The Christian walk is all about balance, and all of either studying or reading will leave you unbalanced. If you are unbalanced, then you run an increased chance of stumbling and falling.

Not only is the Christian walk about balance as far as the difference between studying and reading the Bible goes, but there is a balance to be had as far as studying the Bible internally (The many things mentioned in this chapter), and studying some of the various external issues. The next chapter will cover some of these external issues and hopefully give you a good idea of what is out there along with some good reasons for you to go beyond looking in your Bible, but also to look in*to* your Bible and investigate its history and background. In the same way that one gains a deeper understanding of who a person is when they begin to explore where they come from, their cultural roots, their family lives, and their geographical origins, so is it also true that these background type investigations help one grow deeper in their understanding of the Bible and, thus, in their relationship with God. So, without any further delay, let us make way to chapter 3.

CHAPTER 3

Going to the Beach

All the things mentioned in the previous chapter are internal aspects to studying the Bible. The word study, topical study, and verse by verse study are all focused on examining the content of the Bible. External study focusses more on studying the context of the Bible. If internal, content study is swimming in the vast oceans of Scripture, then external, context study is like walking the various different beaches of the world. Earth has one large body of water called the World Ocean. The World Ocean, however, is divided up into many "oceans"—the Atlantic Ocean, Pacific Ocean, Indian Ocean, Arctic Ocean, and the Southern Ocean. If we were to walk the shorelines of these different oceans, there is much we could learn about that ocean. This is sort of a crude analogy to external Bible study; we learn about things in the Bible by studying the surroundings of the Bible. Historical issues, cultural issues, background issues, archaeological issues, all of these are external issues, but they nevertheless play a huge role in confirming and understanding the Bible, and communicating what it teaches.

Background Bible Study

It has been my experience that many people lack knowledge and understanding concerning the background of the Bible—what it is, where it comes from, who wrote it, when it was written, what the culture was like, and so on and so forth. For whatever reason, whether it is lack of guidance from a mentor, lack of leading from their pastor, or simply a general lack of interest, these people stop at the internal study. This is bad because it leads to an unbalanced understanding of the Bible's content—and balance, as we noted before, is key for progress in the Christian walk. Learning about external features and facts strengthens not only one's understanding of exactly what the Bible is, but it truly helps build and strengthen one's faith because it helps them realize that the content of the Bible is rooted in the actual history of the very world we live in. Many times we take this for granted on principle, but digging into external Bible study truly helps bring the reality that the Bible reports on real people living in real places at real times to the forefront of one's study and one's faith.

Considering that, and going back to my statement about most people not knowing what the Bible really is when they start reading it, I think when you begin to study the Bible externally, you realize how much you don't actually know about it; that helps you develop a respect for its vastness. Aside from that, in order to best understand the message the Bible is communicating, we need to understand the world which it is communicating from. Of course, I could be wrong about your level of understanding regarding what the Bible is and the world and culture it comes from. Maybe you know a lot about this topic, but just in case you do not, I will go over some basic things you might encounter on an external study.

Different Perspectives: Mark and John

The most obvious thing I think people need to realize, is that the writings in the Bible are the individual works of multiple authors written at separate times. You've got all these people, either witnesses or close associates of witnesses, who thought it good to record their experiences, or the experiences they received testimony about. So you have, for instance, the works of John, and then the work of Mark. These represent a different perspective and position of authorship. John writes an eyewitness account from his own experience of walking with Jesus, and he tells us exactly why he is writing, "So that you may believe that Jesus is the Christ, the Son of God; and that believing you may have life in His name (NASB)."[1] Mark, on the other hand, is not an eyewitness. But rather, "It is generally agreed that Mark received much of the information in his gospel from Peter."[2] But how do we know this? It is precisely because even though there is no verse in the Bible that offers this information, external studies of other ancient texts and traditions provide the information.[3]

When we read, things can seem a lot more flat and two-dimensional if we don't know anything about the background. Consider this perspective presented by both Mark and John. Internal study shows Mark's accounts sought to present a balanced view between Jesus's divinity and his humanity.[4] John also sought to draw attention to both Jesus's divinity and his humanity, but external evidence shows that John's motivation to teach about Jesus's humanity was to combat the false Gnostic beliefs beginning to develop at the time John wrote that taught Jesus was never truly human.[5] Understanding John's reasoning for his position truly adds depth to his words; it helps bring us into the world from which he wrote.

Luke: The Historian

Then we have Luke. His work is unique in that Luke is neither an eyewitness, nor is he drawing from one major eyewitness source. Luke acts more as an investigative reporter. He travels, he investigates, and he interviews. However, like John, Luke gives an explicit explanation for his work,

> Inasmuch as many have undertaken to compile an account of the things accomplished among us, just as they were handed down to us by those who from the beginning were eyewitnesses and servants of the word, it seemed fitting for me as well, having investigated everything carefully from the beginning, to write it out for you in consecutive order, most excellent Theophilus, so that you may know the exact truth about the things you have been taught (NASB).[6]

According to Luke, he is writing so that we can know our faith has been placed in true and historical events. A read through Luke's writings reveals that he seems to include many details which when researched can provide historical credence to his work. Take, for instance, the fact that he includes so many details about Zacharias and Elizabeth.[7] Maybe we cannot verify every detail, some things are just lost to the sands of time, but the simple fact that many details can be verified even 2000 years later stands as a testament to Luke's attempts at providing a historically accurate and verifiable account.

The background information and external study truly shines, however, in that they verify the situation described by Luke. What I'm talking about is the fact that Zacharias was chosen by lot to go into the temple and light the incense. External studies show this to be how the whole system would have worked at the time Luke describes. But it goes even further than that. External study provides the information that there was such a large number of people in Zacharias's clan that his serving in the temple would have been a once in a lifetime occurrence.[8]

Since this information isn't directly mentioned in the Bible verses, this is a perfect example of how external study adds to what we can get from our Bibles. When Luke provides the accounting of Zacharias in the temple being informed by the heavenly messenger that God was about to be working through him and his wife, knowing that this was the only time in his life Zacharias would be there doing this in the temple adds to the awesomeness of the whole situation—and understanding that Luke describes these events taking place exactly how they historically should have is a clear indication of his proximity to the events.[9] In other words, because of external study of first-century history, the reader can be confident that Luke writes from the right place and at the right time in history. When these pieces line up, it adds to Luke's credibility that he is likely to be accurately reporting the more personal aspects of the events to us—such as the exchange between Gabriel and Zacharias.

Jesus

When it is all said and done, the Christian faith all rests on the reliability of our information about Jesus. If he wasn't real, or if he wasn't anything like what the Gospels portray him as, then our beliefs are truly unsubstantiated; there is no substance to our faith if Jesus isn't real, or if he isn't really who we think he is.

Keeping with that thought, this is another big area external study helps us understand and have faith in the Bible. For instance, there are at least five extra-biblical mentions of Jesus.[10] That is to say five separate writings from non-Christian sources that talk about the historical Jesus of the Bible. I'm talking about ancient Roman, Jewish, and Greek texts, official and historical writings, confirming the reality of Jesus. This is huge because it grounds Jesus's life, for people who have trouble trusting the Bible, in historical documents found outside the Bible. No other religion, no other supposed holy book, no other belief, and no other faith, to the best of my knowledge, has this kind of outside support.

Also, it goes so much further than simply confirming Jesus's existence. External sources provide information that proves the Bible to be accurately describing the life and times of the Greco-Roman world and specifically the life and times of first-century Palestine in such a way that even many of the individual stories of Jesus's life are supported by external study. Aside from the Pool of Siloam where Jesus heals a blind man in John 9:7, and the Pool of Bethesda in John 5:2, external evidence has also located Jacob's well where Jesus meets with the Samaritan woman in John 4:1-42.[11] These are just a few of many examples, like the discovery of giant foundation stones such as Jesus likened himself to in Mark 12:10, houses with thatched roofs such as the one in Mark 2:4, and giant millstones like the one Jesus references in Matthew 18:6.[12]

Perhaps even more interesting, we can visit places such as a plateau in Galilee where one man could stand elevated and because of special acoustics deliver a speech to a vast number of people, like Jesus did in the sermon on the mount (Matt. 5-7). Also, looking out over the sea of Galilee, one could observe the nighttime torches of the hilltop city of Hippos such as Jesus may have been when he made his statements about a city on a hill not being hidden in Matthew 5:14. Or perhaps Jesus looked down at the Kidron Valley with its newly dug tombs when he accused the Pharisees of being like whitewashed tombs in Matthew 23:27.[13] All of this valid and relevant information comes from external study, and far from simply confirming the Bible, it adds depth, beauty, and a sense of reality to our study. Like I said, it takes the picture of a flat and colorless, two-dimensional view we have of these events, and it changes that into a robust, full, and live-action vantage.

Abraham and the Old Testament

Now, so far I have been mainly speaking of the Gospels—the records of Jesus's life, his words and deeds, and his death and resurrection. These are in the New Testament, which is primarily about the birth, growth, and outcome of the Christian Church. The Old Testament deals with how God chose a people to represent him, their course throughout history, the ongoing prophecy of the coming Messiah (Christ in Greek), and the general thoughts, emotions, and character of both mankind and of God.

You probably knew all that, but it gets interesting when you consider and keep in mind that Jesus, for instance, only had the Old Testament. The obvious reason is that the New Testament hadn't been written yet. If you take this same concept and keep playing it further back in time, books of the Bible drop off one by one because they too hadn't been written yet. I say all this to point out again one of the most fundamental truths about the Bible— it is a collection of works. All these works are different. Many are different styles, and many are by different authors. There is poetry, prophecy, origins, record keeping, testimonials, letters of instruction, and more.

Apart from these literary functions, the more one gets to know about the culture and the time, the more they can understand what is going on in the writings. When we in the United States read, we are ultimately anchored to our modern, North American understanding of life. This hurts our understanding of the Scripture because we tend to read our own understandings into the words of the Bible. What I'm trying to say is that when we know little or nothing about the culture from which the writings come from, sometimes we can think they are saying things that they were never actually saying or doing things they were not actually doing. This really hit me during my Old Testament studies when I examined Genesis and the life of Abraham.

In Genesis 16, we read that Abraham and Sarah decided it would be good to have Hagar, Sarah's servant, be a surrogate mother for Abraham's child—since Sarah was barren. In our modern mindset, many think this is such an appalling and abominable action (Abraham sleeping with his wife's servant). Now, there clearly were problems with this, and certainly some negative outcomes. However, when one looks into the culture and customs of the times, it was a perfectly legal and legitimate thing for Abraham to procure an heir through one of his servants. In that sense, "Ishmael was born, a full and legitimate son of Abraham by the customs of the day."[14]

This is just one example, but it truly opened my eyes to the fact that we can totally misread something when we do not understand its historical context. In our modern time, Abraham's actions would be morally unacceptable for many. To be sure, they certainly went against God's plans even then—in other words, I'm not saying the Bible condones or promotes this. Simply put, however, Abraham was just doing what his cultural setting deemed appropriate for a man in his position. If not for external study, one misses this and the account comes across as something a lot different than what it actually was.

There are uncountable verses in the Bible where misunderstandings could happen, and do happen. This is why the informed person will always have a better chance at understanding what the Bible is actually saying and teaching, and it is also why one should desire to be such an informed person. Obviously not everyone is called to be a historical scholar, but thank the Lord that some people are. Those of us who are not on that level of academic research and study can greatly benefit from the work of the people who are. By using the tools mentioned in the previous chapter (Study Bibles, Bible dictionaries, and Commentaries), even a casual reader can build up over time a good background knowledge of at least first century Jewish culture (to understand the New Testament), but also the times and cultures of previous centuries in order to help us understand the various books of the Bible as they go further and further back in history.

Conclusion

Knowing these external features helps our understanding when we are studying internally. That's why it is good to read whole books of the Bible. If you blindly jump from the middle of one book to the middle of a different book, you will most likely be getting a completely different person from a completely different time, who could be living in a different culture and talking about something completely different. This is how mistakes in interpretation, understanding, and application happen. If we understand the lives and times of the people, however, we can make distinctions between, for instance, the culture of David and the culture of Paul.

As a final word on the subject, I just want to say that I understand how all of this can seem overwhelming. Try not to worry about it all at once. There is just no way you can learn all this stuff in a short time. Christianity is not a sprint, it is a marathon. You have to pace yourself—reserve your energy and have conditioning and control. It is perfectly okay to not get everything. I believe because of grace and because of the indwelling presence of the Holy Spirit, that God brings us through the early times when we don't know much.

Both the apostles Paul and Peter make reference to being spiritual babies. This isn't an insult, but rather a revelation. Peter says, "Like newborn babies, long for the pure milk of the word, so that by it you may grow (NASB)."[15] Newborn babies need milk to live and to grow; they are not yet ready to eat solid food with substance. Paul uses this same idea with the Corinthians when he says, "I gave you milk to drink, not solid food; for you were not yet able to receive it (NASB)."[16] All this is to say that God understands there is a time when we are not yet fully developed in Christ. In fact, I would say none of us ever become fully developed in Christ in this life, but we do grow. This growth is the whole point the writer of Hebrews is getting at by saying, "Everyone who partakes only of milk is not accustomed to the word of righteousness, for he is an infant. But solid food is for the mature, who because of practice have their senses trained to discern good and evil (NASB)."[17]

So again, don't worry if you can't imagine learning all of this right off the bat—there is a time for milk. Just take it slowly, one meal at a time, one mile at time, and one day at a time. God will see you through—but don't forget, while there is a time for milk, there is also a time for meat. There will come a day where just a basic foundation of biblical knowledge will not be enough to bring you through the challenges of your walk. With that in mind, enjoy the milk, enjoy the easy stuff, but don't forget there is always a next step in your journey. There is always a new level of study for you to embrace, there is always a next phase in your Christian growth to step into, and there is always a deeper level of intimacy for you to experience in your relationship with God.

As we consider that, and as we search and swim the deeper waters, we must be aware that the deeper the waters, the greater the risks (Not that we should be afraid). So moving into the next chapter, we will examine some of the proposed troubles involved with a deep and thorough study of the word of God. And we will come out on the other end equipped with the tools necessary to understand that there truly is nothing to fear about a deep and rich study of the Bible. Our faiths, along with the faith of a great many scholars and theologians, remain not only unshaken, but also strengthened and reinforced by a sound study of God's word. Onward we must go, then, into the deeper waters to face together whatever we may find there!

CHAPTER 4

Watch Out for Sharks

Keeping with the swimming motif, and as I have said in the previous chapter, plunging the depths of the Bible is more like swimming in the ocean than it is swimming in any kind of man-made pool. The problem with the ocean, despite all of its wonder and beauty, is that it has dangers. I'm not saying that reading the Bible is dangerous to your health, quite to the contrary. There are, however, predators when it comes to the critical world of Bible study. These predators do not tend to go after prey of their own size and strength, as most predators do not—that is to say, in a very real way the people who take issue with the Bible do not tend to attack ones who can defend themselves—but they tend to target the weak and ill-equipped. The general public, with little to no education on the Bible, and the otherwise unbelieving population, who are always looking for more reasons to justify their unbelief, are the target of atheistic propaganda and skeptical scholarship. These spiritual sharks swim around the ocean of Scripture and tear apart anything they can.

Now, I can tell you that upon fair investigation of many supposed issues, nothing has shaken my faith in the Bible. In fact, the further I go in my education, and the more I investigate the attacks made against the Bible, the stronger my faith in its inerrancy, authority, and inspiration becomes. That is the very blessing I hope to pass on here. This chapter will glance at the tumultuous topic of various attacks on the Bible in hopes of helping you see the kinds of issues out there and the types of responses sound biblical scholarship provides so you too may both take comfort that there are solid and substantiated responses to the seemingly weighty accusations, and also so you can be equipped to respond should you encounter them. It should be said, however, that this is not a self-defense course in defending your faith. This is simply a stepping stone to help you see what some of the attacks are and sample the defenses we may take up.

Charges Against the Bible

There are many false charges leveled against the Bible, for obvious reasons—or perhaps it is not so obvious. The simplest thing I can say about this is that some people just do not want to accept what the Bible says, so they look for reasons to reject it. You are unlikely to hear anyone say, "I really want to believe in the Bible, but I just cannot because of all the errors and contradictions." No, it always seems to be someone who, based on their preconceptions and worldview, already rejects the Bible but now needs a reason to substantiate their pre-decided rejection. Now look, there are endless reasons people cite for not wanting to believe the Bible. A whole book could be written on that topic alone, and true enough many have been, but here I will pick out just three popular points to discuss. These lies are spread around on the T.V, on campuses, and even in some liberal churches, as if they were indisputable and proven fact. Of course, I guess that is the standard for all lies. The real fact, however, is that none of these slanders are true. I don't just say that because I am a follower of Jesus Christ and I'm supposed to say and believe that either (Not my style). I can say that these are false charges because I have done research and Bible study to verify that these accusations against the Bible are simply not true.

A lot of what we talked about already will build up your trust in the Bible. Internal study will help you see there are really no errors and contradictions, and external studies will help you realize that because of the dates, authorship, and authenticity of the ancient documents making up the Bible, there was no heavy editing or other authentic gospels. So that's what we will discuss. First, that the Bible is supposedly full of errors and contradictions. Second, that there are numerous other "gospels" that are equally relevant but are not included in the Bible for malicious reasons. Third, that there was heavy editing, so we don't have a reliable copy of the Bible. All of these claims are false, but each of these claims are used to stump, belittle, and berate unsuspecting Christians who earnestly try to share their faith with others. So, let us look at them a little closer, and you can decide for yourself what you think.

Contradictions and Errors

This is perhaps the most generic attack on the Bible, and while these shots are often fired, they are always shooting blanks. I use that reference because this is a very deceiving argument on behalf of the "shooter." There is a big bang, and there is a smoking gun, but there is no penetration because there is no actual bullet. Let me explain. We already talked about how the Bible is a collection of individual works. So, when you think back to the first century (which is when all the texts of the New Testament were written), you can imagine that all these different pieces of individual writings were being copied and circulated and recopied and recirculated and so on. This was necessary because, first and foremost, the local church bodies wanted to get their hands on as much of the writings as they could. So, all those letters from Paul, Peter, John, and the others in the New Testament were widely distributed. The second reason is more practical; the material used for writing didn't last that long, so they had to keep making copies.

What we have today, are all these ancient copies. Now, brace yourself…some of the copies have mistakes. Wait! If some of the copies have mistakes, then how do we know what the Bible is supposed to say? Because we have the other copies. This is what the field of *textual criticism* is all about. To put it in simple terms, trained professionals will look at all the copies, and when, say, some of the later copies spell John as 'Johnn,' then when compared with the earliest copies who all spell it as 'John,' it is easy to see that the word is supposed to be spelled as John. In other words, "Textual critics specialize in looking at thousands upon thousands of minute differences in the ancient New Testament manuscripts,"[1] in order to figure out what the original text said. The problem peculiar to New testament studies is that all these misspellings or sometimes missing words or letters are labeled as errors in the Bible, but there is no real error. So, when someone states that there are thousands of errors in the texts, while they would technically be telling the truth, they would be intentionally deceptive if they did not disclose that these are all mainly grammatical errors and spelling mistakes, *and* that these errors are fixed by professionals in the printed Bibles we have. Listen, if you are questioning your faith in Jesus Christ because of spelling mistakes, and I truly hate to say it like this, but it is not the textual errors that are the problem; it is your heart.

Okay fine, but what about contradictions? This is much of the same smoke and mirrors, although the illusions get a little more crafty. Whenever I think of the contradiction argument, I always think about the horses. Between 2 Chronicles 9:25 and 1 Kings 4:26, one verse says Solomon had 4,000 horse stalls, and the other verse says he had 40,000. Some people cry contradiction, but is it really that hard to figure out what happened? In the context, we know that there are only a couple thousand chariots, so obviously a copyist scribe accidentally put in an extra zero. These are the kinds of things that are typically pointed out as contradictions, and they are generally very easily explained.

At the same time, it should be noted that there are sometimes *seemingly* genuine contradictions. However, *seeming* like a contradiction to a person thousands of years later who may be taking something out of context, or might have a poor understanding of some ancient cultural nuance, is far from something *actually being* a contradiction— this is one reason why background study is so important. If you put in the time to do research and Bible study, your faith will never be shaken by any "contradictions" in the Bible because there are no unexplainable contradictions to be found. This isn't simply my opinion either; the best and the brightest in modern biblical scholarship stand by the affirmation that the Bible is accurate and inerrant. This is why those who discharge these attacks are shooting blanks; their attack looks real, but when the cameras stop rolling, there was never really any danger.

Before moving on though, I think it would do our conversation well to make plain the point of this particular argument: The skeptic or unbeliever wants to show that the Bible has errors and contradictions in order to demonstrate that it is just like any other piece of human literature. In other words, they want to say it is not the divinely inspired word of God. I point this out to highlight a peculiar turn in the argument. First the skeptic or the unbeliever will insist the Bible is like any other piece of writing, but then they will insist that one must use methods other than the standard processes for judging it. In doing this, the skeptic inadvertently admits what they seek to deny, that the Bible is somehow unique. I shall briefly explain.

In the world of examining ancient literature, there are several principles used by professionals to aid them in their work—and I am not talking about only biblical scholars, but scholars of all ancient history from Nefertiti to Napoleon, to Nicolaus Copernicus. Here are some examples of these principles used to authenticate ancient texts, "The unexplained is not necessarily unexplainable...The context of the passage controls the meaning... Clear passages illuminate cloudy ones...An incomplete report is not a false report...[and] Errors in copies do not equate to errors in the originals."[2] These are some of the graces afforded all ancient texts upon examination—with the exception of the Bible that is. I would contend, however, that one cannot have it both ways. That is to say, either the Bible is special or it is not. It is irrational to insist that first the Bible is not special, but then insist that one must use special standards to judge it by. This is, again, not simply my own opinion, as McDowell concurs,

> In evaluating any ancient manuscript, objective scholars apply a principle that any alleged contradictions in the work must be demonstrated to be impossible to reconcile, not merely difficult to reconcile...Until such time as we have total and final light on any issue, we are in no position to affirm, "Here is a proven error or an unquestionable objection."[3]

With this conclusion, then, let us move on to the next point—while the Christian truly sees the Bible as a holy, special, and unique work, all they ask is that one offer it the same fair evaluation as any other ancient document. On the other hand, while the doubters, skeptics, and opponents of the Bible insist that there is nothing special about it, they also insist that it must be held to some sort of unique standard in judgment.

Other Gospels

The "other gospel" attack is another popular one. This argument states that there are alternative gospels portraying quite a different Jesus, and they were unfairly excluded from the Bible because of their content. Now, much like the error and contradiction argument, there is a certain element of distorted truth to this argument. There *are* other writings claiming to offer more information about Jesus, but the reasons they are not included in the Bible are very different from what popular agnostic or atheistic scholarship would have you believe. Not to mention that, but the entire canonization process is often completely misrepresented in popular writings.

To address that briefly, many think some secret council took place in which power-hungry manipulators picked and chose what writings to include in the orthodox Bible. This is simply not the case. There was never such an individual church council, and although the "official" Bible was decided on at some point, it didn't happen like some would like to portray. The bottom line is that the church body itself decided what they accepted, and this is good because it was the local churches of the first and second century that knew what was authentic and what was false. To be blunt, by the second century, the Church of Jesus Christ was so well established that there really was just no way to sneak in phony writings without them being easily spotted as fake. So, getting to the church councils. These councils simply set in stone what was already accepted as inspired Scripture by the congregations—not the other way around.

So why were the other supposed gospel writings rejected? This is where external biblical study really shines. It all has to do mainly with the dates of the writings. All the New Testament writings are products of the mid to late 1st century. All the other writings that were rejected are from the mid 2nd century on. The trick that is tried by the doubting, liberal, agnostic, or atheistic scholars is to stretch the accepted biblical documents to ridiculously late dates of authorship, and then press the rejected documents back to have equally ridiculous early dates, and, thus, claim them all equally valid. But this is a pipe dream, and a modern issue by modern scholars seeking recognition. This is not an issue that has been pressing since the first century...because there was no issue to them.

You see, to us there is not much difference between something being 1,867 years old, and something being 1,942 years old. To the people of the first and second century, however, there was a world of a difference. Something written in 75a.d or earlier could be easily verified (or falsified) by any of the many surviving witnesses to Jesus's life—such as Peter, John, Matthew, or even their disciples. Something written in 150a.d. or later, on the other hand, is too far removed from the actual events it reports on to have any confirmation or refutation. Therefore, these later writings can literally get away with saying and teaching whatever they want—or at least they would have, but the church was already well established. I guess a man claiming to be God, then rising from his own grave and interacting with over 500 people, and then ascending to heaven in front of some of them has that sort of effect.

The biggest standards, then, for whether a writing is acceptable or not is if they were (a) written in the first century, and (b) written by an apostle or close apostolic associate. This is why so many get excluded. Sure, the fakes try to attach apostolic names to their work, *The Gospel of Thomas*, or *The Gospel of Peter*, but the dating doesn't add up, the details don't add up, and the doctrines do not fit. It is, thus, very easy to spot a fake—unless you don't want *any* of it to be true anyways, then whatever brings a profit is worth pushing. This is exactly what is happening here, as Dr. Craig Evans, established professor of biblical studies, states,

> The problem, though, is there are so many people pursuing doctorates, writing dissertations, pursuing tenure, and trying to get published that there's a tendency to push the facts beyond where they should go. If you're hoping to get on the network news—well, news has got to be *new*. Nobody is going to get excited if you say the traditional view of the gospels seems correct. But if you come up with something outrageous…then that warrants a headline.[4]

The fact of the matter is that these other writings were, and are, rejected for good reasons.

The Bible and its specific exclusivity is a towering enemy to the diverse and subjective worldview promoted by postmodern philosophy. It is, therefore, irrelevant to its attackers whether or not their attacks are based in true and verifiable facts—as long as they can float the argument, get some press, sow some doubt, and sell some books. After all, most people who aren't Christian (and even many who are), lack the drive and the training to really investigate any of these false claims. This is why I am trying to give you a little background, as well as some leads to follow; I want you to be able to check this stuff out for yourself so you don't have to just take my word on it. This is also exactly why I said that external studies of the Bible build your faith. So, as far as the issue of these supposed alternative gospels go, I'll let Dr. Evans have the final word,

> The New Testament writers reflect the testimony of the first generation church, which very much depended on the testimony of Jesus' own handpicked disciples. To take second-century diversity and exaggerate it, and then try to smuggle those controversies into the first century…is just bogus. Real historians laugh at that kind of procedure.[5]

Heavy Editing by the Church

Before getting into this final argument, I just want to make a statement regarding really all of the arguments you may encounter. I don't want to be unfair in my presentation of them, so I will say that at the top of it all, there are some really intelligent and educated professionals who make these arguments. Generally, however, when the average person presents one of these objections, they really don't know what they are talking about. They hear something, they like what it says because it aligns with their worldview or their specific view on the Bible, so they repeat it as if it were verified fact. I guess we can all be a little guilty of that sometimes, but the problem with these false claims about the Bible is that when a top tier professional refutes a claim against the Bible, those on the other side do not seem so quick to send out the memo. So, while in many cases the attack gets a lot of press, the response is usually not publicized very well. I wish this wasn't so, but it is often true. The devil is a liar and a thief, and, as the old saying goes, "there is no honor among thieves."

Now, as we consider this argument, the argument that early church scribes intentionally altered the texts for theological purposes, keep in mind that if you really understand the first two arguments, then you already know the end of this argument. In other words, this argument is also based on real findings, but it is also presented in a way which distorts the truth and thus becomes a lie. The argument is that the manuscript texts were changed and molded for theological reason as the centuries passed, so the Jesus we know today is basically invented; there is no way to know who the original Jesus really was. The analogy most often used is the *telephone game.* You know, where somebody gets a message whispered in their ear, they pass it in a circle around the room, then the person at the end says out loud what they heard so the whole room can laugh at how different it was from the original message. This is the basic accusation against the Bible, with the exception that the church is accused of *purposely* changing the message, in addition to any accidental changes that may have occurred.

The biggest flaw in this argument is that we are not dealing with whispers being passed along for hundreds and hundreds of years. We have written documents. So, as Dr. Daniel Wallace, professor of New Testament studies at Dallas Theological Seminary, says, "If each person in the line wrote down what he heard from the person in front of him, the chances for garbling the message would be remote—and you'd have a pretty boring game!"[6] Dr. Wallace isn't the only professional in the field who thinks the telephone game analogy breaks down. Dr. Craig Blomberg of Dallas seminary says that comparing the Jesus-traditions to the telephone game is completely irrelevant to how it actually happened.[7]

So, we know these texts were not accidentally changed, but were they intentionally changed? The answer is yes, sometimes. But just like in the other arguments, this fact has been completely blown out of proportion. And I don't want you to have to take my word for it, so I'm going to go back to what Dr. Wallace said on the subject when talking about what the most common types of intentional changes are. He says, "For example, the church started using sections of scriptures for daily readings. These are called lectionaries. About 2,200 of our Greek manuscripts are lectionaries."[8] So we have a couple thousand of these portions of Scripture that were modified for daily readings, but since they are hundreds of years old they count as ancient manuscripts, and they were intentionally modified. Given these facts, one can make the accusation that the church intentionally changed the Bible. Now, knowing the details, it is easy to catch the deception in the accusation, so I want you to see exactly the kind of changes these lectionaries had, and Wallace goes on to provide that,

> In the Gospel of Mark, there are eighty-nine verses in a row where the name Jesus isn't mentioned once. Just pronouns are used, with 'he,' referring to Jesus. Well, if you excerpt a passage for a daily lectionary reading, you can't start it with: 'When he was going someplace...' The reader wouldn't know whom you were referring to. So it was logical for the scribe to replace 'he,' with 'Jesus' in order to be more specific in the lectionary. But it's counted as a variant every single time.[9]

The truth is, there is no irreconcilable editing that changes the message of the Bible. Now, that doesn't mean that people haven't tried, either for honorable reasons or not, but the biggest hole in this argument is that we have such a vast number of manuscripts and such a reliable process of dating them, that all the biblical scholars and textual critics have to do is look at the earlier copies to get the original wording—which is exactly what happens when piecing together the Bibles we all hold today.

Conclusion

The ultimate argument is that the Jesus we know is a fairy-tail; if we had the original writings, we would see that we worship an embellished myth. But this is a fantastic stretch of what any actual evidence might suggest. This, like the others, is a pipe dream. It is an example of blind faith on behalf of the skeptic and their preconception that Jesus was just a guy. It's no surprise that all of these theories and ideas presuppose atheism, but it is rather surprising to see how far some of these supposed scholarly authorities will go to justify their rejections of the Bible. This is the main reason I have chosen to use reputable scholars to answer these arguments. And while I don't expect you will be memorizing this stuff, and I don't pretend to have given you exhaustive presentations of these arguments, I did try to give you enough so that you can see the possibility of responding to the accusations made against the Bible with legitimate and verifiable information. Keeping with that, I'll let the final answer to these objections and arguments come from Dr. Edwin Yamauchi, archeological expert and professor of history at Miami University, who says, "The orthodox view of Jesus still stands as the most credible portrait when all the evidence is considered, including the corroboration offered by ancient sources outside the New testament."[10]

CHAPTER 5

The Pure Waters of God

I love drinking spring water. It's funny too because when I was younger, I kind of looked down on the whole idea of bottled water. There are certain kinds, however, that as I grew older and tasted, I found a crisp and refreshing drink that was different from the tap. You have to be careful though because not all bottled water is spring water, and not all spring water is the same. First, there is a difference between spring water and purified water. Spring water is fresh and crisp and natural, while purified water, although perhaps not a bad thing to drink, is run through a purification process at some plant somewhere.

Now, I'm not positive of the whole bottling process and all of such, but for the point of my illustration here, the spring water is the pure product straight from the source, while the purified water is a product of man's engineering. As it relates to the Bible, we all have to ask ourselves sooner or later, "Is this really the pure waters of God, or is this just a product of man's engineering?" In other words, is the Bible God's word, or is it just the work of men? So, having gone through some of the basic arguments and objections people have to Christianity and the Bible, I think it might be a good idea to talk about the fundamental Christian belief concerning Scripture. Let it first be said that whatever you believe about the Bible will ultimately decide how effective your study is in changing your life and drawing you closer to God. Not that your belief changes the Bible at all—no matter what you believe about the Bible, it either is or it isn't the inspired, inerrant, and infallible word of God—but if you do not trust that it is in fact God's revelation to mankind, then you won't really place much weight to any of its teaching. This will be especially true when that teaching goes against something you want to do or have been doing. So even though what we believe about the Bible does not have any effect on the objective reality concerning the Bible, it does have a heavy effect on how one responds to what it says.

I am of the persuasion that the Bible is the Word of God, and so are many others, but there are some—even some who call themselves Christians—who do not believe this to be the case. Nevertheless, the Bible actually makes the claim of divine origin for itself in a number of ways, perhaps no more clearly than in 2 Timothy 3:16-17, which states, "All Scripture is inspired by God and profitable for teaching, for reproof, for correction, for training in righteousness; so that the man of God may be adequate, equipped for every good work (NASB)." Of course, if you don't have a high view of the Bible (that it is God's words to mankind), then you can simply brush this verse off as the words of men.

This is why every Christian must make a decision sooner or later. And the reason I say sooner or later is because I wouldn't necessarily place that burden on a person's salvation, it is the shed blood of Jesus Christ that pays for our sins and brings us into right standing with God, but even a saved Christian can make a real mess of their life, their testimony, and their walk with God if they do not regard the Bible with the proper respect it deserves. If you reserve the right to pick and choose which parts of the Bible you take seriously, then it is ultimately *you* who is leading yourself through life—*not God*. Because the Bible claims to be inspired by

God, and because many portions of the Bible claim to be God's very words to mankind, when we decide to have a low view of Scripture (That it is simply written by men and not God), then we effectively reject those claims. But rejecting the word of God as God's words does not make it any less true. From cover to cover the Bible affirms that it is either recording exactly what God said, or it is ordained and preserved by God to speak for him. This is why God says to Joshua,

> Only be strong and very courageous; be careful to do according to all the law which Moses My servant commanded you; do not turn from it to the right or to the left, so that you may have success wherever you go. This book of the law shall not depart from your mouth, but you shall meditate on it day and night, so that you may be careful to do according to all that is written in it; for then you will make your way prosperous, and then you will have success (NASB).[1]

God is saying that making his word central in your life is good for you. The same basic message is found in Psalm 1:1-3,

> How blessed is the man who does not walk in the council of the wicked, Nor stand in the path of sinners, Nor sit in the seat of scoffers! But his delight is in the law of the Lord, And in His law he meditates day and night. He will be like a tree *firmly* planted by streams of water, Which yields its fruit in its season And its leaf does not wither; And in whatever he does, he prospers (NASB).

God also says his word has power in Jeremiah 23:29, "Is not My word like fire?' declares the Lord, 'and like a hammer which shatters a rock (NASB)?" And not only is it powerful, but it is alive according to Hebrews 4:12, "For the word of God is living and active and sharper than any two-edged sword, and piercing as far as the division of the soul and spirit, of both joints and marrow, and able to judge the thoughts and intentions of the heart (NASB)."

The word of God also asserts its power to cause growth; 1 Peter 2:2 says that we should, "Like newborn babies, long for the pure milk of the word, so that by it you may grow (NASB)." 2 Peter 1:21 states again that the word of God is in fact God's words, "For no prophecy was ever made by an act of human will, but men moved by the Holy Spirit spoke from God (NASB)." And finally, in Revelation 22:18-19, the word of God is final and complete, "I testify to everyone who hears the words of the prophecy of this book: if anyone adds to them, God will add to him the plagues which are written in this book; and if anyone takes away from the words of the book of this prophecy, God will take away his part from the tree of life and from the holy city, which are written in this book (NASB)."

All those verses were just a select few to display that from one end to the other, the Bible is self-aware, it has a high view of itself, and it demands that we also have a high view of it. It's kind of a hard thing to get your head around, and anybody who tells you it is simple or to just accept it, isn't coming from the right place in my opinion. It's okay to wrestle with the Bible and its teachings, but it is also important to know when to submit and to surrender. This is, after all, how we come to realize these wonderful truths for ourselves. So let's dig in a little bit and see what we can discover about the Bible's claims to be God's word.

Just a Book Written by Men

Perhaps you may have heard it said, or maybe you will hear it in the future, that the Bible is nothing more than a book written by men. Of course, if this were the case then the Bible would be no more valuable than any other book for teaching us about God, about ourselves, and about how we should live our lives. But it can't be ignored either, that there is a certain element of truth in this claim. Any text-book, commentary, teaching, or other form of biblical instruction seeking to convey real Bible truth will honestly point out that the Bible was in fact written by regular human beings. This is, of course, a dynamic issue, one truly worth of an in-depth study—an in-depth study that simply isn't possible in my writing here. I think, however, that I must at least attempt to lay the foundation because every Christian should consider the implications of the nature and authority of the Bible.

Many works on the subject start from the top down, that is, that the Bible is God-breathed. I thought I would start with the fact that the Bible is a book written by men. As one concise text-book puts it, "The Bible, like other books, was written by people in specific historical situations, in specific geographical places, and in specific cultural settings that influenced their thinking."[2] In other words, as another text-book puts it, "The human authors were personally involved in the process."[3] In many cases, the writers were recording the things that happened to them and their nation. In other cases, the writer may be writing to a group of people regarding specific issues or in response to previous correspondences. There is also at least one instance where one person writes directly to one other person about a specific and personal circumstance (Philemon). All this is to say, "The Bible was not written in a social and historical vacuum;"[4] the writers, were, to varying degrees, personally invested with what they penned.

Even the most superficial reading of the Bible reveals that it explores human interests; it does so while reflecting human emotions, and in a wide range of human languages and literary styles and forms including poetry, narrative, parables, allegory, symbols, similes, metaphors, and more.[5] To put it very simply, as Dr. Norman Geisler, distinguished professor of apologetics, does, "Like all other books in the world, the Bible had human composers."[6] Sometimes this fact is avoided or neglected when considering the Bible, probably because many skeptics and critics express the fact as an attack. It can't be avoided though; the Bible is a human work from cover to cover. Of course, as noted in previous chapters and previously in this chapter, the Bible explicitly claims to be the word of God. Therefore, while it would be wrong to deny that the Bible is written by men, it would also be wrong to say that the Bible is nothing more than a book written by men. "Its writers claim divine inspiration."[7]

Written by Men, Inspired by God

To say the men who wrote the Bible were inspired by God has a very specific meaning. For instance, even though I feel God has put it on my heart to write this book—even that he is inspiring me to do so—what I mean when I say that isn't what the Bible means when it says it is inspired by God. Which, as it were, is probably the best place for me to go because when I say the Bible is inspired by God, I am not offering my opinion of the Bible. Rather, I am offering the Bible's opinion of itself.

There are two primary sources for this proposition. First, 2

Peter 1:20-21 says, "But know this first of all, that no prophecy of Scripture is a matter of one's own interpretation, for no prophecy was ever made by an act of human will, but men moved by the Holy Spirit spoke from God (NASB)." Here, when it says men were moved by the Holy Spirit, we could think of a sailboat being moved by the wind in its sails as a crude analogy.[8] Next is the Apostle Paul's words in 2 Timothy 3:16, which says, "All Scripture is inspired by God and profitable for teaching, for reproof, for correction, for training in righteousness (NASB)." In summary of these two verses, Dr. Geisler says, "While Peter speaks of the message originating with God, Paul says it becomes the written Word of God."[9]

Now, if these were the only two verses that spoke of the Scripture being the words of God, I would personally feel like that might be somewhat of a flimsy case, given the gravity of the claim. The reality, however, is that there are hundreds of Bible verses which point to God as the ultimate author. Consider how Zechariah 7:12 speaks of, "The words which the Lord of hosts had sent by His Spirit through the former prophets (NASB)." One could make a short-list of Moses (Deuteronomy 18:18), David (2 Samuel 23:2), and Isaiah (Isaiah 59:21), where the Bible says something akin to God putting his words in the mouth of these people.[10] There is also the many instances where a prophet will declare, "Thus says the Lord," or, "The word of the Lord came to me," such as in Jeremiah 2:1-2. Then, there is the simple fact that many times the Bible plainly claims, "God said," such as in Genesis 1:3.

"Another way," According to Geisler, "the Bible claims to be the Word of God is expressed in the formula 'What the Bible says, God says."[11] He goes on to explain that many times a saying will be written as the words of God in one place, "God said," but then when the same saying is referenced later, the Bible says, "Scripture said it."[12] In this sense, Scripture saying something becomes synonymous with God saying it. This isn't highly selective either; all throughout the New Testament, the words of God all throughout the Old Testament are recorded as the words of Scripture. From one end of the Old Testament (Genesis 12:3, quoted in Galatian 3:8) on through (Isaiah 55:3, quoted in Acts 13:33-34), and so many places all over, the New Testament quotes the words of God as the words of Scripture. This is all to point out that the Bible through and through views itself as the very words of God.

The divine inspiration is by far not the easiest concept to comprehend. It is, however, somewhat straightforward, as one instructional text explains, "Biblically and theologically, then, inspiration refers to the influence God exerted over the human writers of Scripture. By inspiration, He guarantees that the result accurately expresses that which he intends to communicate."[13] The Bible is God's message and instruction to mankind. So, while the men who penned the verses of Scripture were personally invested and involved, as previously stated, "Their product was the result of the work of the Holy Spirit in inspiration."[14] In this sense, being the very words of God, "The Bible not only has a unique message, but it claims authority from God with that message."[15]

The Authority of God's Word

It stands to reason that if the Bible really is God's word, and God really is all mighty, all powerful, all present, and all knowing, then his words are the final authority on any issue. This is why it is important to know, not just believe, that the Bible is in fact God's inspired word. If you have any doubt in that, then you will not respect its authority. The authors themselves, even though many of them were unaware that they were in fact penning God's word, viewed all of God's previous words with authority, particularly the Torah (the first five books of the Bible), which is what Jesus, Paul, and the rest of the New Testament writers speak of every time they use the phrase 'Law.' That being said, much like how the divine inspiration of Scripture is the Bible's claim of itself, so too is it the Bible's own claim to have divine authority.

2 Timothy 3:16, as noted, says that the whole Bible is from God. The application Paul gives, however, speaks not just of Scripture's source, but of its authority. God's word, according to Paul, is for teaching, reproof, correction, training, and equipping. This implies its authority. I cannot teach, correct, or train my son unless he respects my authority; it is a necessary requirement for these actions to take place. The same is true of the Scriptures; they must carry the very authority of God in order for the Bible to be the ultimate source of teaching, correction, and training.

In one way or another, the Scripture either declares or implies that every word is God's choice, the tenses of the verbs, and even whether a noun is plural or singular are all specifically ordained by God; even the tiniest part of every letter, according to Jesus (Matthew 5:18), belongs to God.[16] This is extremely important to understand regarding the authority of the Bible because if God is intimately involved in even the tiniest little mark of every letter, if every single part or aspect of the Bible is there on God's purpose, then we are responsible to obey and respect all that the Bible teaches. In other words, we don't get to pick and choose what we like and then leave the rest.

"The inspiration of God," as Dr. Geisler explains, "extends to every part of Scripture, including everything God affirmed (or denied) about any topic."[17] If one understands that the Bible is fully inspired by God, then they cannot sidestep the fact that "the omniscient God cannot be wrong about anything He teaches or implies."[18] This is the Bible's authority simply put. Of course, one may wonder how far God's authority goes in regards to other writings claiming to deserve or having been offered a place in Scripture. This is why the guidelines mentioned in chapter 4 are important to remember—that the historical dating and authorship of each writing has everything to do with its qualifications to be included as Scripture.

I say this to address the fact that some versions of the Bible include more books in it than others. These extra books, however, do not carry God's authority because they are not inspired by God. That is not to say they hold no academic or literary/historical value, but for various reasons, they should not be considered Scripture. This is noted here because the main issue on these books—the deuterocanonical and apocryphal books included in some Bibles—is whether they carry with them the authority of God-breathed Scripture, and the answer is no; they were not written in the times they claimed to have been, and they were not written by the people they claim to have been written by. For these two main reasons, and others as well, these books should not be considered Scripture, and thus should carry no authority on matters of doctrine and practical issues of faith. "No other source equals or surpasses that of Scripture; the Bible alone, is a supremely authoritative book in matters of faith and practice."[19]

Inerrant and Infallible

Finally, as we near the end of our brief examination of what it means to declare the Bible is inspired by God, we must look at the declaration of inerrancy and infallibility. In short, if the Bible is

God's word, and God is all knowing and is the final authority on all things, then all of Scripture is inerrant and infallible. But what does this mean? Simply put, it means that the Bible is true and without error. If you remember, however, when discussing some of the accusations made against the Bible, we acknowledged that some of the many manuscript copies had errors in them. How then can we say the Bible is without error? The answer lies in what we hold to be inspired by God. It is, after all, only what comes from God that we can guarantee is inerrant and infallible.

Plainly stated, then, "Inspiration guarantees only the accuracy of the original writings, not of later copies or modern translations."[20] In other words, "Copies of the original are only inspired insofar as they are accurate copies of the original."[21] For this reason, it actually does make a difference what translation of the Bible one reads, or better stated, it makes a difference whether one has a good translation of the Bible or not. I will go over this more in the next chapter, but for now it can simply be stated that the guarantees attached to a God-breathed Bible are only valid when we are actually getting the words God breathed out.

We can be thankful, then, that God providentially protected the copies to such a degree that their standard of accuracy is "exceeding 99 percent."[22] This isn't simply an opinion or wishful thinking either. As one writer puts it, "The science of textual criticism has proven what we would expect if God is continuing to watch over His Word: That the degree of accuracy with which the biblical text has been transmitted is fantastic."[23] So, far from simply a tradition or dogmatic belief, the claim that we have today the same words penned by the original writers is based on a scientific evaluation. Of course, like many other instances, this scientific evaluation is simply pointing to what the Bible has been stating all along, that God's word is faithful to endure.

TREVOR WAYNE ROLLS JR.

So, again, what about the errors in the copies? I only bring this up because learning that some of the manuscript copies have errors can make a person extremely uncomfortable if they are not familiar with the inner workings of the topic. I think many people are unaware of how we get our Bibles, so they have never investigated the topic of manuscripts, copyist errors, textual criticism, or anything else on the subject. Therefore, to ease any potential discomfort, I wanted to take a moment and pass on these few facts concerning copyist errors,

> No original manuscript has ever been found with an error in it...
>
> Errors are relatively rare in copies... In most cases we know which wording is wrong from the context or parallel passages... In no case does an error affect any doctrine of Scripture... Errors don't affect the central message of the Bible.[24]

All this considered, and even thought, "Divine inspiration and inerrancy, therefore, applies to the original text, not to every detail of every copy,"[25] we have good reason to accept the certainty with which Christians claim to possess divinely inspired Scripture.

Confident that we have God's word, then, what are these guarantees we may attach to it? First, "Inspiration guarantees the events presented as historical to be historical; to really have happened, and in the way described. Inspiration also guarantees that God included them for a purpose."[26] Far from being a God of confusion, the God of the Bible wants his people to know him, to know his creation, and to know the path to salvation. So, even though there are some doubters, skeptics, or flat out opponents who are working overtime to put forth their belief that even if there was a God, that God would be unknowable by mankind...

74

the Bible's "inspiration does guarantee the truth of all the Bible teaches, implies, or entails (spiritually or factually),"[27] precisely so that mankind can be sure not only of the fact that there is a God, but also that the God of the universe wants to be in an intimate relationship with his creation.

All that being said, there are several things that inspiration does *not* guarantee. Dr. Geisler has compiled a list of those things which I will pull from in order that you might get the general gist of what inspiration does not guarantee,

> It does not guarantee that every part of a parable is conveying a truth (as opposed to the truthfulness of the point the parable is illustrating) ... Nor that no exaggerations (hyperboles) can be used... Nor that all statements about the universe must be from a modern astronomical perspective (as opposed to a common observational standpoint) ... Nor that truth is exhaustively revealed or treated (as opposed to adequately presented) in the Bible...[28]

This list isn't exhaustive, but it gives a general idea of the types of things inspiration does not guarantee, which, I would add, fall in line with what one would expect from any ancient, non-fiction work.

In other words, the Bible openly uses round numbers, parables, poetry, figures of speech, observational language, hyperbole, and more. Therefore, the Bible remains to be invariably true as long as one fairly considers these facts—as one would with anything else. For instance, when the weather forecaster on the morning news predicts tomorrow's sunrise to be at 5:45 am, nobody seeks to discredit him by pointing out that the sun doesn't actually rise... for he is using observational language which we all use. To this point, Dr. Geisler concludes his list of things the Bible's inspiration does not guarantee by saying, "Everything the Bible affirms is true, but what is meant by truth must be understood in light of the phenomena or data of Scripture."[29] That is to say, within the contextual confines of the truth which it claims, it's claims are true.

Conclusion

The main thing to consider when trying to wrap your mind around the inspiration, inerrancy, and infallibility of the Bible is that it has a dual nature. Much like the living Word of God, Jesus Christ, the written word of God has a human aspect and a divine aspect. This is, for instance, why the truth conveyed in the Bible is from a phenomenological, observational perspective. Each writer, of their own free will, wrote what they wanted, how they wanted to write it, and when they felt the inclination to write it. At the same time, the divine nature of the Bible is that, "God in His providence engaged in a divine concurrence between their words and His so that what they said, He said."[30]

There are, it should be noted, two extremes that various groups, denominations, and religions fall between, and both should be avoided. First is the extreme that the Bible is solely divine, and second is that the Bible is solely human. Neither of these work well in practice and both are a heresy to put forth. The truth is not necessarily easy to wrap one's mind around, but it is simple to state: The Bible is not *either* God's word *or* man's words, nor is it *neither*; the Bible is *both*. How God worked this out is not known, but the fact remains that he chose to use men who chose to be used in delivering mankind God's word of instruction. The Bible's "primary cause," then, "is God, but its secondary causes are human beings, and although the Bible is the Word of God, it is also the words of men."[31]

I have relied so heavily on outside sources for this chapter because I want to offer you a quality explanation of such an important truth for the exact reason that it is such an important truth. As I stated before, what you believe about the Bible will ultimately dictate how seriously you take its commands, instructions, doctrines, and truths. And honestly, if the Bible is not the Word of God, then who cares about what it says? But the Bible is God's word, whether we like it or not, and it, thus, holds the highest authority about life, reality, worship, religion, and our relationship with God—there is simply no way around this, and it is true whether you or I believe it or not. Now, since I leaned so much on the work of Dr. Geisler to deliver the truth about the inspiration of the Bible, I will let him have the final word on defining it,

> Inspiration is the supernatural operation of the Holy Spirit, who through the different personalities and literary styles of the chosen human authors invested the very words of the original books of Holy Scripture, alone in their entirety, as the very Word of God without error in all that they teach or imply (including history and science), and the Bible is thereby the infallible rule and final authority for faith and practice of all believers.[32]

CHAPTER 6

Broaching the Tide of Translation

There is much to be said on the topic of Bible translation—much that is generally unknown by the average person. It takes, as with any topic that is dynamic or difficult, a bit of research to get your head around the gist of the subject. But it is a worthy cause. The Bible is our handbook, as it were. It is meant to be read, and it is meant to be understood. In this sense, then, a person needs to acquire a Bible they can read and understand. Unfortunately, there can be a lot of dogma, tradition, opinion, and general laziness involved in which Bible translation a person reads. My goal here in this chapter is to try and remedy some of that for you. I am not going to declare that one translation or another is the only translation a person should read, nor am I going to declare that every translation is sufficient. I do, however, want to pass on some of the information I have come across on the subject over the past few years of my academic study.

When I really get into something, whatever that may be, and whatever area of life it may be in, I find that understanding the details of the inner workings and finer points help me to grasp the issue as a whole. This is true for me when I do auto-mechanics, music recording, or instrument building; this is true for me in my karate study, and in my academic study. Understanding as much as I can about what I am involved in is one of the keys to success in all the things I do apart from my biblical and theological studies. It is, therefore, a very reasonable conclusion to draw that understanding everything I can about the inner workings of issues within theological and biblical studies will prime me for success or maximum benefits from those studies. This, however, is often not the case with the average Christian, in my opinion. Bible study, prayer, and devotional time often fall to the wayside in the lives of believers. You can figure this out by regularly attending a study group and seeing how many people take the time to pre-read the material, do a little background research, or simply be bothered to remember what was taught the previous week. And the funny thing about it is that most of us seem perfectly okay with knowing next to nothing about what we are banking our eternity on.

I have never been able to be that person in my walk with Christ. The Lord delivered me in such a profound and powerful way, and he continued to do such amazing healings and transformations in the lives of myself and my family, that I can't help but have a burning desire to learn as much as I possibly can—to be the best disciple I possibly can be—in order to draw as near as I possibly can to the one who has done so much for me. This doesn't mean I think I am perfect. This doesn't mean I don't make mistakes, slip into ruts, embark on the occasional Netflix binge, but it does mean that at the root of my faith is a desire to know my Savior, to know the Father, and to know the Bible as best I can. And this means, yes, suffering through some dry historical or academic studies sometimes. But I figure it this way, if Jesus can endure six hours of suffering on a torture stake, as well as the beatings, lashings, and humiliation leading up to being nailed to that cross...then I can sacrifice some of my precious Netflix time in order to learn more about him, about God, and about the Bible.

Understanding the Issue

When I was younger, well before I became a Christian, a person was likely to respond to the question of if they read the Bible by saying something along the lines of, "I would read the Bible, but it is so hard for me to understand with all the thees and thous." This of course is referring to the King James translation of the Bible (KJV) and is a reflection of the fact that, "The KJV for a long time was the most widely used translation in the world."[1] This is because, "It also served for several centuries as the classic expression of the English language."[2] My opening statement, however, also reflects that those days are long since passed by; the English used in the King James Version, known by many as Elizabethan English, no longer effectively communicates to the modern, English speaking world. That is not to say that nobody can understand it, or even that many cannot understand it; it simply means that the language used in the King James Bible is just not how the average person speaks on a day to day basis—and this is taxing on the reader. I'm not saying this to attack the KJV, but rather to simply point out the basic need for more modern translations.

What is a translation? The answer probably seems obvious— you take something from one language and say it in another language. To understand better what is happening, however, a few fundamental terms and points should be explained. Essentially, the process involves someone, or a group of people, who are adhering to one of several *theories of translation* in order to communicate words, thoughts, and ideas across historical, cultural, and, obviously, language barriers from an *original language* to a *receptor language.* Many who do not understand even these fundamental terms and processes, simply put, do not understand translation, and somebody who does not understand translation is likely to think it simply involves finding the coinciding word in one language to match the word from the other—and sometimes this is the case—but language and expression of thoughts and ideas in written form can be much more complicated than that.

Many languages use devices such as masculine or feminine nouns and perfect or passive verbs, or other such tools to indicate subtle details. These devices, however, are not present in all languages. For instance, Greek, the language of the New Testament, uses these devices while English, the modern American language, does not. Considering just this one example, you can see how a person responsible for completing the translation would need to command a mastery of both the original language and the language receiving the translated message in order to effectively communicate the subtle details conveyed by the literary tools of the original language to the actual words and phrases needed in the receptor language. This linguistic expertise is of course of utmost importance, but linguistic analysis and textual criticism will not be the main focus of this brief exploration of the translation process. Instead, I want to focus on what I believe is the most important issue for the average person to consider—*translation theory.*

It should be said before we move on, however, that in the thick of it all, mastery of the languages and mastery of several areas of manuscript study (the sciences involved with studying the actual ancient documents) are probably the most important things to consider on the scholarly level. The reason we will not look so much at those here is because it is few and far between that translation projects do not employ the best and the brightest linguistic, historical, and textual scholars from a myriad of denominations as well as perhaps even skeptics and agnostics (for accountability reasons), in order to ensure quality and reliability in the finished work. Most translations out today, particularly the better ones, keep detailed documentations and records of just who is on their translation teams for the very purpose of accountability, being examinable, and being transparent to the questioning world. It is, therefore, not the priority of this type of work to look much into that, even though it is possible. We can justifiably trust in the linguistic ability of those involved with many modern translations. The more important issue, especially for the layperson or average reader, is what translational theory the scholars are using as a guideline.

Theory of Translation

The theory of translation employed by the translators of your Bible will basically have everything to do with why it reads the way it does. This is why I think it is the single most important thing for the everyday Christian, the one who doesn't have the calling to dig extensively deep on a scholarly level, to know about their Bible translation. Being educated on this one area sort of cuts through most of the history, tradition, and dogma to get at the most relevant issue for the modern American Bible student. To sum up, then, what *translation theory* means; it is the method, intention, and outcome the translator desires. This will be understood a little better when I explain the various theories.

Formal Equivalence

When I hear the word formal, the first thing that comes into my mind is a formal event—tuxedos and gowns, and that sort of thing. This, however, is not the idea that *formal equivalence* is trying to convey. Rather, it is "The attempt to keep as close to the 'form' of the Hebrew or Greek, both words and grammar, as can be conveniently put into understandable English."[3] The syntax, the style, the sentence structure, even if it is completely unfamiliar to what modern readers are used to seeing, is sought to adhere as close to the original *form* of the ancient writing as possible—hence the term *formal equivalence*. This theory literally "seeks a word-for-word translation from one language into another."[4] In that sense, these translations, such as the KJV, NASB, or HCSB, seek to give the reader the exact words in English that the original authors penned in Greek, Hebrew, or Aramaic—wherever possible, of course. One can certainly appreciate the value of this.

However, there are certain draw-backs as well. As mentioned before, the modern world just doesn't communicate in the same way as the ancient world. We structure our sentences differently, and quite simply, we use different words to express ourselves. In this sense, even if one gives us exactly the words of the apostles, prophets, and preachers, we may not *understand* what they are saying. It simply isn't possible for a translation of this type to "communicate every linguistic and cultural particularity with clarity and precision."[5] At first, one may be somewhat put off by the idea that translators can't accurately tell us what the original authors were saying, but you should know, that is not what I am saying at all.

Simply put, even though there is great value to the formal equivalence translation, when it comes to things like wordplays, idioms, words with various shades of meanings, and things like monies and various units of weights and measurements, translating word for word does little to bring understanding to the mind of the modern reader. It would be just as difficult if one were to take a chunk of modern America, perhaps a newspaper or magazine, and translate it word-for-word into ancient Greek and send it via Doc. Brown's DeLorean back to 1st century Palestine with the expectation that people would understand fully what they were reading. Could we really expect them to understand what a "twerk" or a "Twitter" is? Of course not! The translation would have to be a bit more explanative in order for them to get the picture; it would do better to include the *function* of the word in addition to simply the *form*.

Functional Equivalence

The theory known as functional equivalence seeks to get past the communication problems of the formal equivalence previously mentioned. It is "The attempt to keep the meaning of the Hebrew or Greek but to put their words and idioms into what would be the normal way of saying the same thing in English."[6] Sometimes people call this a thought-for-thought translation. The idea being that the translator seeks to capture the thought of the original author while feeling like they have a little marginal freedom to express that thought in the receiving language. For that reason, when these translations are read in English, they often feel a bit more free-flowing and easier to read and understand. Departing from the restrictions of a formal theory to adopt a more functional theory leads one to what we might call a *dynamic equivalence* theory. These translations include versions such as the NIV and the NLT, and they are very popular in many modern, evangelical churches. They feel a bit more natural, a bit more modern, and, well, a bit more American. This is because they are dynamic; they move and flow with the receiving language. Where the formal translation favors the original language, the functional translation offers more to the receptor language.

The obvious drawback here is that while these versions are easier to read and understand, we are putting more trust into the hands of the translator to really be giving us what the original author was saying, since they are not tasked so much with providing the exact wording. In essence, the translator, when giving us a functional equivalent, is, as the word implies, not seeking the *form* of the original writing, but the *function*. The danger is that they are making what we call exegetical and interpretive decisions along with their translations.

This is where the importance of having a committee comes into play, as noted by Drs. Fuhr and Kostenberger, "While translators will inevitably be involved in interpretive decision making, there is a hedge of protection from theological prejudice as Bible translation committees typically represent a variety of ecclesiastical traditions and theological positions."[7] This helps with the fact that "Scholars have been known to let their pet theories and traditions interfere with their sound judgment."[8] Not just scholars either, we are all bound to what we have previously accepted and traditionally believe, at least to some degree. However, having to present one's conclusion to twenty, thirty, or forty other critically minded people of equal training and sometimes opposite traditions helps check and balance the exegetical and interpretive decisions of a single translator so that we are getting a rational and reasonable translation and not a homiletic commentary. It is always easier to float unreasonable ideas by those who follow closer to your line of reasoning than it is to get them by people who approach similar topics from different angles. Thus, we can be thankful for the brilliance of one having to present their dynamic translation before a diverse committee.

Free Translation

A free translation sort of captures the same idea as free-hand drawing—looking at an image or thing and trying to draw it with your own hand without using measurements or instruments to guide your work. Essentially, then, you are just trying to capture the idea of the source material, but it is run through the filter of your own brain. In this sense, the end result of your free-handed drawing represents more so how *you* view the original drawing rather than an effort to accurately reproduce the original. This description very much so applies to free translation. In fact, another way of expressing the idea of free translation is to refer to it as a paraphrase, and another way of describing a paraphrase is putting it in your own words. A good example of this is *The Message Bible.* In this case, the passages are very free-flowing and easy to read because the author exercises the right to mold and shape the words and phrases into their own words in order to communicate the message.

Of course, some might rightfully wonder where the value is in a Bible that is not seeking to give the original wording or thoughts of the biblical writers, which is a valid concern. The value, I think, comes in the fact that renditions such as this present an easy to read, general idea of what the Bible's message is. In many ways, the free translation is on the opposite extreme of the formal translation. Not to downplay its significance, but as an illustration; if formal translations represents tuxedos and gowns, then free translations would be more like a pajama party. Even so, to give a scholarly perspective on its benefit, Fee and Stuart say, "These editions sometimes have especially fresh and vivid ways of expressing some old truths and have thus served to stimulate contemporary Christians to take a new look at their Bibles."[9]

Whatever good can come, however, they also point out the biggest concern with paraphrasing the Scripture, "A free translation can easily become too free—reflecting how the translator wishes the concepts would have been conveyed, rather than reflecting faithfully how they actually are conveyed in the original text."[10] If this were to happen in the translation of a committee based functional equivalent, the committee would discuss and debate the interpretation until they agreed on what most accurately represents the original thought. This, however, is not the case with paraphrases. There is no "hedge of protection," because there is no committee.

When this is the case, when one person writes a paraphrase of the whole Bible, "You will subject yourself extensively to the exegetical opinions of the translator."[11] Whatever dogma and traditions, whatever denominational preferences the paraphraser holds ultimately becomes incorporated into the writing and presented as what the Scripture actually says. In paraphrasing the writer can end up "departing in large scale from the vocabulary and grammar of the original text."[12] Based on these reasons and others, Fuhr and Kostenberger conclude that "While these may be helpful supplements for Bible study, you shouldn't use them as primary translations for study or regular reading of God's word."[13] Fee and Stuart add that this is a fact even the ones doing the paraphrasing "would be quick to admit."[14]

If it isn't broken

I think that having options regarding what translation of the Bible a person reads and studies from is truly a good thing. There are many, however, who do not agree. They have become very attached to some of the older translations, and they adopt a position that sort of says, "If it isn't broken, don't fix it." It truly is an important issue for some who would even break fellowship or look down on people as a sub-par Christian if they use certain translations or don't use certain translations. Others do not take it to this extreme, but still feel there is something amiss in the newer translations and, therefore, it would be best—in their opinion—if people stayed with what has been used in the past.

I was recently part of an online discussion with a friend of mine who holds a different opinion than I do on the topic of translation (I know it is crazy in today's world to entertain the idea of remaining friends with someone who holds a different opinion than yourself, but all things are truly possible in Christ who strengthens me), and because of this I got to hear some of the concerns and arguments of truly God-honoring Christians who are against new translations. By the way, when I say new, I mean within the last hundred years. The very same last hundred years that have shown remarkable leaps in areas of science, archaeology, medicine, mechanics, engineering, and so many other areas that God has blessed humanity with progress, but many believe still that biblical studies is best served by using the tools of the past.

On that line of thinking, it has been said that we ought to just stick with the traditional texts—since they have served the church so well in the past. It has also been said that there being so many modern translations is a device of the devil to divide and break down the church. Another angle of approach is that the scholarship who produces these translations are all just as sinful and misled as the rest of us can be. On the other end of that, it is said that every Christian possesses the same Holy Spirit that these scholars are indwelt by and therefore should have their opinions on things such as Greek and Hebrew language, textual criticism, and historical and archaeological studies held with the same weight as the scholars. Finally, and relating to the last statement, it is pointed out that in modern times, the average person has access to massive amounts of information concerning historical biblical studies, and is, therefore, just as able to engage in a conversation on it as trained professionals in their respective fields are.

Most of the examples I just mentioned, I should point out, do contain certain elements of truth. In the end, however, I do not believe they warrant an abandoning of using modern Bible translations. I will, therefore, examine and explore these claims, in order that we might together see where they lead. Of course, it is obvious and prestated that I do not agree with what has been said in rejection of using new translations, nevertheless, whether one agrees with a position or not, that should not stop them from investigating its claims. This is what true critical thinking and honest scholarship is about. It is also how the average person gets a good handle on an issue in order to make an informed judgment for themselves, which is the point of this exercise—equipping *you* to make an informed decision so you don't have to rely on others to make the decision for you. So then, let's look at these claims together.

Back to the Traditions

In a long thread of debating, eventually it was said that we should just return to the traditional texts since, after all, they have proven to be effective over the years. This is sort of like saying, "If it isn't broken, then don't fix it." Now, the first thing one needs to do is figure out what a person means by "traditional text." Without having to put much thought into it, one easily arrives at the conclusion that the King James Translation is what the person has in mind. I don't want to spend too much time on this, since tearing apart the King James Bible is not my intention. It has served as a mighty tool in the hand of God to spread the gospel for hundreds of years—about four hundred years to be exact. That being said, if you consider the words and deeds of Jesus, Peter, Paul, Luke, and all the other people of the New Testament were in writing before the end of the first century, then you have to wonder how Christians read the gospels before 1611 (The accepted year of the King James Bible)? The answer is that they read the Bible the same way we do today, by usage of translations.

In fact, many would argue that Jesus, Peter, James, Paul, etc., were themselves using a Greek translation of the Hebrew Scriptures known as the Septuagint.[15] This would have been the result of Hellenization—the spread of Greek culture and language throughout the ancient world. It is noted that even hundreds of years before Jesus was in Jerusalem, the Jews had become Hellenized to the degree that they were copying the Scriptures into the Greek language because many were no longer fluent in their native Hebrew language.[16] It is also a considerable thought that, "The Gospel writers were actually involved in some level of translation as they composed their inspired texts, as Jesus and his disciples were likely speaking Aramaic, yet their words are presented in the Gospels in common, everyday Greek."[17] Finally, far from simple assumptions, "Most of the citations of the [Old Testament] in the [New Testament] are from the Septuagint."[18] All this is to point out that translation was part of the process even from ground zero.

As the traditional line continues up through time, the Septuagint ended up becoming the main translation of Christianity, along with the Greek New Testament.[19] It also was the translation of which most other translations were based off of. This persisted until about the 5th century when a Christian named Jerome decided to translate the Scriptures into Latin. "What made his work unique was that it was not based upon the Greek Septuagint version but upon the actual Hebrew of the original Old Testament."[20] Now, this is important to note because when Jerome had finished, there were certain differences in some of the exegetical choices he made—based on different, older and more authentic, source texts. The problem, however, is that Christians were so used to the Septuagint that it was controversial to have another translation where words might vary.

Metzger tells of the new version being rejected in Africa because Jerome chose to use the word *ivy* instead of the previously used word *gourd*; Metzger describes Jerome's choice of words as an "unfamiliar rendering."[21] It is important to note here that Jerome was not wrong or inaccurate, but that what he chose was unfamiliar. As White recounts the early Christian leader Augustine's reaction, he notes that Augustine's complaint was not having anything to do with the quality of Jerome's translation, but rather, that peoples "ears and hearts have become accustomed" to the Septuagint translation.[22]

All of this is to note that throughout history people do not like change, no matter how much better the change may be. In the case of the Latin Vulgate, "opposition to the revision subsided, and the superior accuracy and scholarship of Jerome's version gave it the victory."[23] Of course, then a most peculiar thing happened. Over the next eleven hundred years, the Latin Vulgate became the most widely used Bible across Europe; "It held the position in the minds of Christians that the Septuagint had held a millennium before."[24]

Just like with the Vulgate and the Septuagint, however, as time pressed on and new needs arose, it eventually became apparent that the Vulgate translation was no longer the best tool for the job. So, much like how by the time Jerome began translating into Latin, there was already a large amount of sub-par Latin translations in existence—hence the need for a good one—[25] the same scenario came about regarding translation into English as we come forward in time to the King James Version; from the Wycliffite Bible, to the Coverdale, to the Geneva Bible, and several in between, a polished English translation was needed.[26]

The King James Bible truly was a treasure of its time, but to bring this all back around to the topic of our discussion, in each case a new Bible was introduced there were many who thought it best to stick with the "traditional" texts, the older and more familiar renderings. Many might say, "If it ain't broke, don't fix it!" In each case, however, *it was broke...* There was a need for these new translation, but the traditionalists could not or would not see it, and the average person simply had a hard time accepting something that was new or different. Even in the case of the King James Version, which in many ways was a superior translation of its time, we see that people were not eager to accept it. Metzger notes that the Puritan Pilgrims who came over to America on the Mayflower, as well as King James himself stuck with the Geneva Bible.[27] It seems the traditional view would be to reject whatever is new for whatever is already accepted; it is, I think, in our nature. However, just like with all the translations before it, "As times passed, expressions of dissatisfaction with the King James Bible began to be replaced by the growth of approval for the version."[28]

So now again, as time has passed (400 or so years) times call for updated tools. But much like in the past, there are many who resist the change and cry out for a sustaining of the traditions. But also like the times before, the traditions are broken...and in need of fixing. It is, then, like White says, "There is nothing wrong with tradition as long as we do not confuse tradition with truth. As soon as we become more attached to our traditions than we are to the truth, we are in very deep trouble."[29] And the truth of the matter when it comes to the traditional King James Bible, is that even though it was one of the best works of its time, times have changed.

Fee and Stuart note that the source materials used for the translation of the King James Bible are "late manuscripts which had accumulated the mistakes of over a thousand years of copying."[30] Fuhr and Kostenberger take it a step further by pointing out that "Modern advances in New Testament textual criticism, including discoveries of literally thousands of Greek manuscripts that were unknown at the time of the King James translation, as well as computer technology used in the study of Greek manuscripts, demand that modern translations carefully consider all available manuscript evidence in determining the Greek text that most accurately represents the original."[31] This is a hugely important point in the discussion because as we covered in the chapter on the inspiration of Scripture, it is only inspired and authoritative inasmuch as it communicates the original words that God gave. This means that as the receptor languages change, translations must be updated to maintain an accurate reflection of the original message.

So what do we do with this? Many out there feel deep convictions about the King James Bible. Many feel like the traditions have served us well, that God used the traditional texts to do wonderful things over the past 400 years. I would agree with that, but I would agree that it is because of God's awesomeness that he was able to do wonderful things with less than the best—as is always the case. Mankind never brings a perfect offering, but God always does a perfect work. In the case of Scripture, as I have shown, what we have only gets better as time passes, and as God blesses us more and more with a deeper, richer understanding of his word. None of the scholars I have used in this discussion think a person should not appreciate or even read the King James, or any of the other older Bibles, for their sentimental or even poetic and devotional values. However, they all offer similar views to Fee and Stuart who insist, "For study you should use almost any modern translation other than the KJV."[32]

Too Many Translations

Another strong opinion about English Bible translations is that there are just too many of them. As noted above, some think this is a demonic tool to divide, dishevel, and disillusion the church. Perhaps there is something to this, although I am inclined for the most part to think not. It is easy for us to always assume the worst, but I think that it is far more likely a saturation of the word of God in the world is a plan from above than it is a ploy of Satan. Now, I'm not saying the devil does not get his hand in on the action—especially when he sees an opportunity to sow discord— but God's authority and sovereignty is so far above the evil hearts of mankind, and even the vileness of the devil and his dark legion, that even among any small pockets of darkness in the seas of God's word, the vastness of his light is not even nearly matched…nor will it ever be. Not to simply write off the argument, however, let us look and see. Let us ask together, why are there so many translations?

First, we covered one main reason already—theory of translation. Some believe a formal translation is the best approach, while others believe a functional approach best gets the job done. And, again, even others think a paraphrase serves the world best.

All of that approach deals with the process, the method, but what about the material? As we just discussed, many believe the manuscripts used for the KJV represent God's word best. Yet there are others who think we have better and older manuscripts that better give God's word. How do we hash this out? We undertake translation projects and compare the results. Another reason demonstrated is that languages develop and grow. The source languages, Greek, Hebrew, and Aramaic will never change; they are dead. The receptor languages, in our case English, is always growing and changing. Therefore, as time goes on, even modern translations become outdated and need revisions. Thus, more translations. Another issue I like to consider is reading level. I read and comprehend very well, but others are not as studied as I am so the Bibles I read effortlessly require from them more effort to read. Should I demand they raise up to my level (as if I am anything special)? Certainly not! Neither does God. In fact, that is the whole philosophical notion behind the coming of the Lord Jesus Christ: Man could never reach up to God, so God came down to man. The same is true of God's word. If you do a Bible-reading-level search on the internet, you will find that some Bibles have a 12th grade reading level while others have only a 6th grade reading level, and yet many others fall somewhere in between. Is this insulting? Absolutely not! In his mercy and grace, God saw fit to make his word available to all, so that whosoever might come would actually be able to read his word and come.

So, as I conclude on this point, are there some Bibles that are better translations than other? Sure. Could there be demonic plans involving how words are translated? I'm positive there is. God, however, is in control of all of this, and whatever evil may be amiss, there is certain goodness flowing from the fountains of God's word. In fact, on a global scale, I think we need more translations.

According to any information I have heard, there are thousands of known languages in the world and there are only hundreds of Bible translations. So, as long as there are people out there who haven't heard the gospel…I say keep those translations coming.

Spirit Filled Sinners in the Age of Information

Here I kind of want to pile the remaining arguments together in order to not drag this out further. In one sense people will say that the scholars are just as sinful as anyone else (implying that those making these new translations are led astray). On the other hand, they will say that we have the same Holy Spirit that they do (implying that we are just as good as they are). Finally, it is said that we all have access to the same information. All of this is true. The implications, however, are in error. In matters of the soul, sin and salvation, yes, the Bible scholar needs Jesus to die for their sins as much as I need Jesus to die for mine. Similarly, yes, I have the same Spirit, the same blessing, the same Seal, and same infilling that they do. But the simple fact of the matter is that I do not have the same training and expertise. Fuhr and Kostenberger write, "For today's Bible student, the most basic tool is a good translation of the Bible in his or her own language."[33] I don't speak Greek, and I don't speak Hebrew, so if I want to know what happened when God entered humanity and paid for my wretched sins with his innocent and pure blood…then I need someone who understands the language to translate that message for me. The apostle Paul writes in his letter to the Christians in Rome, "How then will they call on Him in whom they have not believed? How will they believe in Him whom they have not heard? And how will they hear without a preacher? How will they preach unless they are sent? Just as it is written, "How beautiful are the feet of those who bring good news of good things (NASB)!"[34] To this I would say, how beautiful are the hands that translate the good news into language I can understand!

So yes, we all have the same guilt, the same forgiveness, and the same power. God, however, gave us different gifts and different tasks. It is some people's job for the kingdom to be scholars for the Lord. And it is other people's blessing to benefit from that. The second I start to think I don't need the blessings of those who came before me, or those who walk beside me, that is when I begin to wander away from God's purpose in the body of Christ. The scholars and translators are members in the body of Christ. Perhaps they are hands and I am the feet. Or perhaps I am the feet and they are the hand. But how remiss would a foot be to resent the hand, or the hand to reject the foot? Thank God, then, for translators and scholars to serve his purpose in the kingdom of heaven!

Conclusion

Even though this is the longest chapter of the book, I feel like there is so little that was said. The topic of translations is something that truly fascinates me. Unfortunately, it is a topic that many have little actual knowledge about beyond dogmatics, conspiracy theories, and perhaps a rudimentary understanding. It is a shame! Churches should be equipping the saints for battle in the way that a soldier can completely break down and reassemble their rifle without hesitation. Instead, many churches, for whatever reason, are completely at ease with their congregation, with their unit of Christ's soldier being largely ignorant about the inner workings of their main weapon, the swords of the Spirit—the Word of God.

So what Sword should one take up; what translation should you use? This is the question of the day, and I have avoided it up to now because I never want to be that guy who goes around telling people what Bible is the only Bible God would have them use. I feel this way because God is largely silent on the issue. In short, God has given us choices. But I will share with you what I think is the right approach. First and foremost, understanding the difference between translations is key. This is the reason I went into detail about the different theories. Before I understood the theories, I thought versions like the NLT were terrible because I personally read formal, word-for-word translations. This being the case, I reasoned that if what I read, the NASB, is a literal translation, and the NLT doesn't even seem to say the same things sometimes… then they really missed the mark and it is a bad translation. Now that I understand more about the subject; now that I understand the NLT is a dynamic equivalent, that it was never trying to give me a word-for-word translation, now that I understand the intent of the translator I can respect the mission and read it for what it is.

So as we try to land this plane, let's think of the absolutely most important aspect of Bible translation—getting the original message. There is nothing more important. If you are not getting what the original author said as God inspired them to say it, and meaning what God meant it to say, then you are not getting the inspired and authoritative word of God. We mentioned this before in previous chapters and previously in this chapter. One other thing we mentioned in the previous chapter is that the inspiration of God can go down to the very details of words, or letters, or verb tenses, or singular and plural nouns, and so on. So this is extremely important. The slightest changes can alter the meaning and thus alter the inspiration, so how could I choose anything other than a formal equivalence? Well, consider also that a slight misunderstanding of the meaning of a passage can alter its authority. Perhaps then I should go functional equivalence so I know what it means... You see the seriousness in a person's translational decision? I want you to keep that in mind as we move to conclude this chapter.

Having given you much of what I have to offer on the subject, although I'm sure I could drone on for another twenty pages, I think it would be best to let you see what those with more expertise have to say on the issue. After all, they are by and large where I learned what I know on the subject, so why not give it to you straight from the source. Starting with White,

> Many factors can, and should, go into your decision as you purchase a translation. Whether you like a more literal, formal translation or a more dynamic, free flowing translation will impact your choices. Study editions, companion volumes, concordances, even print style and size are all issues to take into consideration. What translation is predominant in your local church is important as well, especially if you will be teaching or leading Bible studies. But one thing that should never be a factor is intimidation. You should never have to wonder if you are going to be accepted by others if you use an ESV rather than a KJV (or vice versa).[35]

In other words, White is saying that there are several considerations that should be weighed, but being bullied into one choice or another shouldn't be part of the process.

All things considered, then, Fee and Stuart say, "It's probably a good practice to regularly read one main translation, provided it is a good one."[36] "You should realize, however," according to

Fuhr and Kostenberger, "that there's no such thing as a perfect translation, and thus the diligent student of the Bible should utilize a variety of versions."[37] To which Fee and Stuart agree because "The trouble, then, with using only one translation, be it ever so good, is that you are thereby committed to the particular exegetical choices of that translation as the Word of God."[38]

Anyone who has ever been to a group Bible study and played the, "Mine says this," game understands that different translations seem to say different things at times. These are the exegetical choices just mentioned. Many times, and especially if one is uninformed about the hows and whys of Bible translation, then they will assume the worst of the differences. This is the source of many translation conspiracy theories. However, in reality, as Fuhr and Kostenberger explain,

> When opinions differ between translators, and ultimately between translations, there's rarely, if ever, any malicious intent to tamper with the original intent of the author or to undermine the integrity of the Word of God. Rather, differences occur due to legitimate points of view that come into play in the process of translation. Therefore, knowing that there are places where challenges exist in the translation process, it's always to the benefit of the reader to understand as much as possible why a difference between translations exist.[39]

In other words, the differences mean something, and the more we can learn about them, the better we will understand the original message. Therefore, Fee and Stuart conclude, "For study of the Bible, you should use several well-chosen translations."[40] Note that they say well-chosen. White says, "What we find in modern translations is a spectrum extending from the most formal, literal translations to the most dynamic, functional ones."[41] This one factor will make up a majority of why one translation differs from another; one gives the closest opinion of what the words are, and the other gives the closest opinion on what the thoughts behind the words are. Therefore, "A balance between the two systems, formal versus dynamic equivalency, would seem to be the best approach."[42]

My NASB rarely leaves my side; it is my main translation. However, my NIV is always close by. These are my carefully chosen mains. One is known by many as the best literal translation out there, and the other is seen as the best dynamic by many others. They are checks and balances to each other. Sure, I consult a KJV sometimes, and I check an NLT out because in both cases I like to see what they may add to my understanding. Perhaps this seems overwhelming to you—I hope not because it is important. 1st century Palestine is a long way away from us, in many respects, so it should be no surprise that a little work might be involved with learning the Scriptures. But that's okay. The Lord has left us with some wonderful tools, not the least of which are numerous styles of Bible translations. It's okay to own more than one Bible, it just means you're all the more interested in getting to know your savior and your God. So don't be afraid to pick a couple up. Get a King James Bible and see the almost Shakespearian manner that those in the past enjoyed God's word. Then pick up an NIV and see how comfortable it is to read God's word in your native tongue. Then, maybe get something more midway, like an ESV or an NASB so you can really connect with how the original authors were trying to speak. And, all along the way... let God be glorified!

CHAPTER 7

Coming to the Well

That water is central to life is no secret. However, it can easily be taken for granted in the modern world where we have advanced plumbing systems pumping water directly into our homes. We can also simply drive right down to the store and pick up any goods we may be in need of, including clean drinking water. In pre-modern cultures, of the present and the past, however, this is not the case. In these circumstances of living, one must go to the source—a spring, a river, an ocean or lake, or in the case of this illustration—they had to go to the well. In a biblical sense, when we speak of coming to the well, it is easy to think of the account in John, chapter four. This is where Jesus travels through Samaria and stops at a water-well to take a rest. While sitting on the well, known as Jacob's Well, a woman comes to get her daily water supply. Here, Jesus meets the woman directly at her place of need and reveals himself to her, and through her to the whole town, as the prophesied Messiah.

Now, when I say that Jesus met the woman at her place of need, this is of course true in a spiritual sense, she needed the gospel, she needed the Savior, she needed the *living water*; but it is also true in a very plain and natural sense, she had to come to that well to get the necessary water to tend to her daily needs. If you wanted the water that sustained you in your daily works, you went to the well. If you wanted water to drink or to cook with, you went to the well. In fact, the woman essentially makes that very point when she responds to Jesus's offer of *living* water by saying, "Sir, give me this water, so I will not be thirsty nor come all the way here to draw (NASB)."[1] Of course, she was completely missing the point. Jesus was offering her an eternal place in the family of God and in the kingdom of heaven, but she was enticed by the thought of not having to come daily out to the well and carry the water back to her home—which is the main point I really wanted to make about the well; this is where you went to get what you needed in order to do your daily functions.

This is how I want to think about Bible study as we begin to bring all the things already discussed in the previous chapters together. God's word is a key component in our lives, just like water. Also just like water, we can neglect to take in as much of it as we should. This is, of course, because we have so many other options. But back in the simpler times of Jesus and the Samaritan woman, not like there was never *anything* else to drink—they had wines and juices and milks—but in general, if you wanted a drink...you went to the well and got some water. In fact, for everyday living, you didn't wait until you were thirsty; it was a normal part of your routine. You got up in the morning, got dressed, and went to the well for your daily water. Then, as the night drew near, you went back to the well for your evening supply. Similarly, this is what we should do with the Bible; we want to train ourselves to go to it daily for our needs—before the desperation or the dire circumstance actually arises. Imagine the ridiculousness of a person waiting until they were dying of thirst before dragging themselves out to the well? No, we must make regular, daily trips out to the source so we can stay supplied with what we need to live.

Simply going to well, however, isn't enough. Jesus was at the well, but he didn't have the required tool to get the water out, as the woman points out when she says, "Sir, you have nothing to draw with and the well is deep (NASB)."[2] You see, you can go to the well all you want, but if you don't have the right tools to draw the water with, then you can't get anything from the well. The same is true, in a sense, with the Bible. It contains the word of God, the wonderful gospel, instructions for living, for relationship with God, and for relationships with each other; but if we don't come to it with the right tools, it is likely we can make a real mess trying to get anything useful out of it. Now, I'm not saying that the Holy Spirit and the grace of God doesn't cover us along the way as we figure all this out—we have pastors, preachers, and teachers who use their drawing tools to provide water from the well for people unable to draw for themselves—but I am saying that sooner or later, if we want to experience substantial growth in our walk with God, we need to learn for ourselves how to study his word in a fruitful and productive way. We need to be able to draw from the well when nobody else is around to do it for us.

The Tools for the Job, and the Tricks of the Trade

Some translations read that the woman at the well says to Jesus, "You have no bucket." This is very simple and clear, but for the purpose of this illustration, I like how the NASB says "You have nothing to draw with." We don't ever want to come to the Bible without being able to draw from it. So, we are going to explore how to draw out of what we might call the well of Scripture. To do that we need the means, and we need the method. I have worked in several sub-vocations of the construction industry in my life, and if you yourself have become fluent with how to do a particular trade or process, then you know that for every task there are the right tools for the job, and there are helpful tricks of the trade. In other words, in all things you need the right components to make it work, then you need to have the know-how to actually make it work. All of the previous chapters, for the most part, sought to lay out the tools for the job; these are the means. Not that I was exhaustive, but for general purposes I have told you all you should need. Study Bibles, various translations, commentaries, dictionaries, and concordances—all of these are tools for the job. Following, we will discuss the process, the method by which we can use these tools to draw out from the deep well of Scripture life-changing waters of God's truth.

Principle Before Process

Before diving into the process by which we might extract from the Bible, understanding the principle behind the process is essential to success. All of this can become rather academic sounding, simply because the words and phrases are foreign to a person who has never engaged with the ideas before, but for everyone there has to be a jumping off point. Maybe you are a person who knows a bit about what is to follow, and if that is the case then great! However, maybe the things to come are completely new to you. If that is the case, please be patient. I know some of these words may sound intimidating, but I assure you, the function behind the words is very practical. Why we need big words to describe simple things I am not sure, but what I am sure of is that with a little faith, patience, and grace you'll be able to pick right up on this stuff with no problem. Now then…

The underlying principle of authentic Bible study is called the *exegetical principle*. There are other principles that are helpful to be sure, but this is perhaps the one that captures the ultimate goal—to draw from the text what it contains. We call this exegesis. Simply put, exegesis seeks to extract the intended meaning of a text by its original author to its original audience. To do exegesis is to take from the text only what is there. On the other hand, when we read into the text a preconception or any idea other than the intent of the original author, we do what is called eisegesis. The words sound similar, but they mean the opposite. Exegesis extracts from the text; eisegesis injects into the text. If we remember that our translations are only the inspired and authoritative word of God insofar as they communicate the original texts that God inspired the original authors to compose, then we can understand that we are only getting, again, the inspired and authoritative message insofar as we pull from the text what is there. If we read our own thoughts into the text—if we do eisegesis—then we are not getting the inspired word of God. This is why the exegetical principle is foundational to authentic Bible study.

If I truly and authentically want to study the Bible then I want to draw out what it has, not read into it what I think. It is noted by Fee and Stuart that many people only take to exegesis when there is some obvious conflict in what the text says and what modern understanding holds. They insist, however, that intentional exegesis should always be in play, and not just a tool to be used under specific circumstances. To this they explain, "The real problem with 'selective exegesis' is that one will often read one's own, completely foreign, ideas into a text and thereby make God's Word something other than what God really said."[3] We don't want to do that. If we are truly interested in hearing from God, then we must approach the Bible exegetically. Otherwise, we might as well not even bother with the Bible because we are really just interested in our own ideas anyways.

Induction and Deduction

Similar to exegesis and eisegesis, there are two forms of reasoning involved in study—inductive and deductive. For the former, you take all the bits of what is there, in this case the biblical texts, and you form an idea of what it means based off of the information in the text; this is induction. For the latter, you seek to explain what all the parts mean based off of a pre-established idea—deduction. To summarize, induction looks to the text for ideas and explanations, while deduction works from ideas to explain the texts. You should note that induction and deduction are not identical to exegesis and eisegesis, but there are similarities. In exegetical and inductive study, you look to the source for your ideas. In eisegetical and deductive study, you bring the ideas from outside the source. To this it is noted that "deduction is not inferior or negative in and of itself, but for those who seek to discover what the Bible means, an assumption-oriented approach to the meaning of individual texts is counterproductive and impedes discovery."[4]

It should also be noted that while deduction is not necessarily negative, it is often used negatively. As an example, when one uses inductive study, they read in the text of Scripture many accounts of God working miracles, the prophets doing miraculous things, and Jesus doing the miraculous works of his Father. From these readings, we can come to the conclusion that the Christian God is one who works miracles. Conversely, as is done by many skeptics, doubters, and unbelievers, the text is approached deductively with a pre-established notion that, for instance, miracles do not ever happen. Starting from this position, when they read the texts that contain miracles they deduce that these are mythological insertions and legends that have crept in alongside otherwise historical accounts. The conclusion is not arrived at by any means or evidence from within the text, but rather, it was decided beforehand and used to evaluate the text.

It doesn't take much to see that this is not a fair and objective approach to Bible study. The text must be allowed to speak for itself if we are to ever learn from it what it was intended to teach. It is possible, however, that we can learn something from the text inductively, like that it is inspired of God and therefore authoritative, and then use that established, biblical belief in a deductive manner—approaching the text in future study with the idea of inspiration already in mind. In this way, the text has spoken for itself inductively, but we do not have to go and re-establish what we already know before every single reading. As all of this leads into our overall approach, we can see why, even though deduction is a part of the process, exegetical study is one consisting primarily of the inductive method.

The Creative Bible Teacher's Inductive Study Method

Here we will discuss a system laid out in a book called *Creative Bible Teaching*.[5] The book, of course, will take you much further than my simple chapter will, but I can at least give you the keynotes to get you going, and you can decide for yourself if or when you want to dig deeper into further study. Before we dive in, though, I want to clarify a couple things about the creative Bible teacher's inductive study method. First, do not be misled by the word *creative*. It is a theme developed throughout that book dealing with how teachers must be creative in their approach, much like Jesus and Paul were in using whatever changing means were relevant and available to them in order that they might present an otherwise unchanging message to various people groups. Fee and Stuart appropriately explain that uniqueness has no place in the exegetical and interpretive intentions of the Bible student; "That is not to say," they clarify, "that the correct understanding of a passage may not often seem unique to someone who hears it for the first time. But it is to say that uniqueness is not the aim of our task."[6] How could it be, after all, if the correct understanding of any given passage is only ever what the original author, under the inspiration of the Holy Spirit, intended his writing to mean?

Secondly, as we previously touched on, although we call this the inductive study method, it actually does involve deduction as well. Exegetically working to draw out from the text what is there, induction plays an important role. Then as we prayerfully seek to turn what we pulled out into practical applications for our lives, deduction becomes the prime tool of reasoning. This is the part of the study process where it is okay for unique and individualized perspectives to come into play because even though the interpretation can only ever be what the original author intended to write, the application is customized to you and your situations. These two modes of thought, induction and deduction, are both equally essential for going from the then and there of the Scriptures to the here and now of our lives, but care must be taken not to confuse them. To liken it back to the illustration of drawing water from a well, the well shaft is narrow, the process is fixed, and the result is repeatable—this is induction—and it must *always* come first before application; the water must be drawn before it can be used. From the well to the house, however, once the water is drawn, there are many functions, many applications such as drinking, cooking, or cleaning—this is deduction—and it is what we do to apply the Scriptures to our lives. With a combination of inductive and deductive processes, then, we are able to extract from the Scripture what happened in the then and there of biblical history and apply it to the here and now of our modern lives.

Then and There to Here and Now

Most of us, for better or for worse, live in the consistent and constant state of here and now. Sure, we reflect on the past, and we prepare for the future, but for the most part, perhaps mainly by necessity, we all dwell in the here and now. I think the majority of us understand that the here and now is where we all are. The thing we might miss, however, is that we take this here and now mentality into most of everything we do. Perhaps some of us are better at waiting things out, but I think many of us ask ourselves at any given time, "What does this have to do with me *right now?*" Take karate or guitar playing, these things have fundamental essentials that need to be learned and developed before one can ever get to the good, "juicy" stuff. And when we are stuck learning the circle block or *Smoke on the Water*, we might wonder, "What does this even have to do with anything?" But as time passes, if we are good students who stick it out, we always seem to realize how those fundamental essentials fit into the foundation, and how they actually do apply to what I want to do right here and right now. This is a very crude analogy for comparison with Bible study, but it seeks to capture the idea that for many it is a problem to see past the very moment they are in.

Whatever we are doing, we always want to know what it means

to *me*—right now. This is true also when we read the Bible. It is especially true if we have some pressing difficulty or immediate expectation we seek to remedy. We open that baby up with our deepest questions or needs at the front of our mind, we expectantly read a passage and ponder the whole time, "What is it saying to me?" Little do we realize, it isn't saying anything to *you*, because it was not written to *you*. Don't feel bad, it wasn't written to *me* either. It was, in fact, written to specific people groups in specific places at specific times to address specific issues and serve specific purposes. The proper approach, then, when we handle the Bible is not to start right up with, "What is it saying to me?" But rather, we should simply ask, "What is it saying?" Once we figure out what it says, we can then ask the appropriate question, "How does this *apply* to me?" Thus we have struck the essence of the inductive study process.

Just like drawing water from a well to use it in one's house, there is a simple process to effectively draw out from what the Scripture says and apply it to your life. In its simplest form, there are three parts to the process: observation, interpretation, and application. I find the five-part process, however, to be more direct and detailed in exactly how one can get the teachings of Scripture worked into their lives. This five part process is observation, interpretation, generalization, application, and implementation. There are three aspects of this process that coincide with going from the then and there of Scripture to the here and now of our lives. We have observation and interpretation, which represent the then and there. Then we have the generalization which serves as a bridge principle—the connecting truth. Finally, we have application and implementation which represent the here and now. This process serves as a direct line of reasoning that seeks to safely bring God's communication to humanity straight into life application for each one of us. So, now that we have kind of an overview of what we will discuss, why don't we dive right in and look at each part individually.

Observation—What does it say?

Observation seems like it would be a simple enough task. You literally observe what the text says. But like anything else that we do, the main problem is that it is we who are doing it. We are fixated on ourselves, so simply observing what the text says is often polluted by our thoughts of ourselves. We all want God to speak to us, and that's a good thing, but I can't let wanting God to speak directly into my life prevent me from seeing the reality of what God is actually saying. It's like when a person is in a conversation with another person, only, the person listening isn't really taking in what the person speaking is saying because what they are really doing is trying to put together what they want to say as soon as the person talking is finished. This isn't listening; it's not observing. Sure, I might hear some things the person is saying, but everything I hear runs through the filter of me trying to formulate what I want to say when it is my turn. When this happens, the intended message of the speaker often is lost on the receiver because they are not paying attention.

In the same exact way, this is what happens to our Bible study. So how do I get past this? Well, one of the advantages of having a text in front of your eyes, rather than a person speaking to you, is that you can simply read it again. One might be hesitant to say to a person, "I'm sorry, but can you repeat that because I was so busy trying to think about what I wanted to say when you finished speaking that I wasn't actually listening to you…" And with good reason. With the Scripture, however, we can simply back up and read it again; no harm, no foul. In fact, if you remember back to what I shared about Dr. Nugara, one of my professors at Regent University, he insisted that we read our passages several times (I think 40 was the number he used) so that we can become completely familiar with what the Scripture says.

This is what we might call *Active Observation*. Unlike passively observing, I am intentionally observing the text so that I might know what it says. And the more I read the words in the passage, the better idea I get of what exactly it is saying. See, sometimes we get lazy with our Bible reading. Sometimes we are less concerned with knowing what it says than we are with making sure we mark our daily chapter down in our 'Good-Christian's-spiritual-itinerary-of-daily-things-to-do-in-order-to-feel-like-I-am-pleasing-God' list. But when we don't make sure to understand what God has said, we are essentially communicating something like this, "Okay God, I pretended to listen to you today, and now that you are done talking, let me tell you what I have been waiting to say." But when we take the time to read it again—and again and again—until we really grasp what it says, we are communicating to God that we truly do care about what he is trying to tell us.

Now, reading the passage several times is a great start, but there is actually much more to observation than that. At the highest levels of scholarship, the observer would be comparing manuscripts, textual variations, grammar and syntax, functions and implications of the original languages, in depth historical and cultural contexts, and any number of other details. Of course, all of this would be cumbersome and even out of reach in some cases to the average reader of Scripture. What is not out of reach, however, are the questions that motivate these various examinations. What I mean to say is that even though many of us do not have the training and tools to do the same type of extensive observational research as those on the highest level of scholarship, we can at least start by asking the same types of questions. By asking these questions as we continue to review the texts and passages we are studying, we further enable ourselves to detach from our self-centered, here and now mindset, and journey deeper into the actual circumstances, content, and message presented by the Bible.

The detailed questions one could ask when studying an ancient text written in a different language to people in a far different culture are perhaps endless, but for sake of study, I think three main lines of questioning are important. We want to ask setting questions, context questions, and structural questions.[7] Honestly exploring these areas will give the reader a good observational idea of exactly what the text is communicating. This is, again, important because if God reveals himself through the message of the text, then we want to make sure and get to that message as it was originally communicated by the original human author—and by the ultimate divine author, the Holy Spirit.

The *setting questions* are in many ways the most basic questions one can ask; these are the who, what, where, when, and why type questions. In this line of questioning, we want to figure out who is writing and who it is written to. It can also become helpful later in the process to know where both parties are located, and when the events took place. Ultimately, though, the most important thing I think to ask is what and why? Why exactly is the person writing these things, and what are the details of what they are writing? This is where we really begin to get out of our own *here and now* mindset. These are the gateway questions; they open up the doors for deeper study. So, you might be wondering, how could someone hope to get easy answers to these questions? Well, you may not even be aware that the answers could already be in your possession. If you own a study Bible, then the chances are likely that these issues are answered at the opening of each book because most study Bibles out today offer at least brief examinations of these questions.

As one digs deeper in observation, *context* is perhaps the next best line of questioning to pursue. Context is important because it is the basis for communication. Everything has context. From letters to words to sentences to paragraphs to chapters to book, everything communicated is done so in a context. But not only that type of context, proper observation involves looking at things such as cultural context and literary context, as well as the textual context mentioned previously. These all play a part in understanding what is said. Trends and customs of the time and culture will make clearer things that can easily get blurry. Also, identifying the literary style will help establish contextual meaning. Is this a parable, a metaphor, a narrative, or poetry; is it history, apocalyptic or prophetic writing? All of this is important to know. One never wants to make mistakes such as reading hyperbolic teaching as literal commands—or other such mistakes. And, of course, then there is the most basic textual context. What comes before the text or passage, and what comes after it? What is the basic message of the book or passage, and how does the verse or passage under observation fit into that message? All of this can easily get lost when a person simply rattles off a verse that they think applies to a situation in their life or someone else's, but it is very important if we want to read the Scripture as God intended it to be read that we keep the words, verses, and passages in their inspired and authoritative context.

Finally, *structural context* should be considered. As one reads through the passage several times, it is important to note any repeated words or phrases. We also want to look for perhaps a progressive theme that may lead up to a climax. Another question is does the writer make any comparisons or contrasts? All these things start to add up and so it is important to note them. Figures of speech, pivotal statements, cause and effects, all of it is important to be noted in observation. Nothing is in the Scripture by accident, so we shouldn't just gloss over anything. If you begin looking, as I did after learning about these things, then you begin to notice how much you never noticed before. And, as it was with me, once I realized how much I missed, and how much it led me to a deeper understanding every time I notice something previously overlooked, then I began to realize just how much of Scripture that I wasn't actually reading as the authors intended it to be read— which also means I wasn't interpreting much of Scripture the way it was intended to be interpreted at times.

Interpretation—What Does It Mean?

Sometimes a person will say something like, "I don't agree with how they interpret the Bible over there at that church." There's nothing wrong with that statement, if there is in fact something wrong with how the people in question are interpreting the Bible. What many people do not understand, however, is that there really is only one correct way to interpret the Bible. This may be shocking to some, but it is true. If interpretation asks the question, "What does the text mean?" Then, there is really only one objective answer to that question, "The correct interpretation is the one that the author intended the reader to come to understand."[8] In other words, in the same way that we should seek to understand what it actually says, and not *what it says to me*; we should want to understand what it actually means, and not *what it means to me*.

This is the case because words have meaning, specific, detailed, and situational meaning. When communicating, if I say one thing but you think I mean another thing, then you really don't understand what I said. The same is true of the Bible. If God is speaking to humanity through the Bible, then we need to understand the words to mean what God intended them to mean. Otherwise we are simply making up our own meaning… and if we are doing that, then essentially, we are playing God. Now, this is, I think, where the problem with people not liking certain interpretations of Scripture comes from. More often than not, I'm afraid, a person does not like what God has to say on an issue, particularly on issues of how one should live their life, so they say, "I don't like how you interpret the Bible!" But the Bible is not fluid. It says what it means!…and it means what it says. So if everything is cut and dry, then how come there are so many different "interpretations" of how to live according to the Scripture? I'm afraid that is a topic for a different book, but what I can say here is how we might safeguard ourselves from falling into faulty interpretation of Scripture.

In a broad sense, there are three basic rules for correctly interpreting the Bible as we read; the first rule is *continuity of the message*.[9] It should be understood that the Bible teaches in continuity from end to end. For instance, if one were to say something like, "I like the God of the Old Testament better because he seemed violent and wrathful, and awesome, but the God of the New Testament seemed too soft and loving for me," then they would have a major misunderstanding of what both Testaments teach, and of God in general. The reason is that the Bible is continuous in its teaching, and it never contradicts itself. In this sense, we always have clear and concrete teachings to draw from when trying to understand a passage that is coming across as a bit difficult to understand. This unity of the Bible is a guideline to use for the interpreter to not step out of bounds in understanding what any given passage of Scripture means.

The second rule of interpretation is understanding *context*. As noted by many capable Bible teachers, "One of the dangers that Bible students must avoid in the interpretation of the Bible is 'Scripture twisting'...taking a text out of context in order to make it say something we want it to say."[10] Ultimately, the Scripture is very efficient at saying what it means. Just like any other form of communication, context is king. If we read the Scriptures contextually, and among their proper place within the passage, the page, the book, the testament, and the Bible as a whole, then it is difficult in most instances to go wrong from the intended meaning. It is when we start plucking little verses and phrases out to use them in whatever way suits our message, or advice, or situation, this is when we run the danger of stepping outside of God's authority. A good tool of contextual interpretation is a scholarly commentary. What I mean by "scholarly" is not necessarily saying it has to be a textbook-like curriculum in the Scriptures, but just that it is focused on the intended meaning of the original writers of the text. Otherwise, there is what we might call a homiletic commentary, which might seem easier and more enjoyable to read, but these are more like sermons focused on telling you what the author thinks of the passages and how they apply. A good scholarly commentary will essentially abstain from this, and seek to focus on issues of language, literature, and culture in order to accurately explain what the text was intended to mean in its historical, cultural, and literary context.

The third basic rule of interpretation is establishing *customary meaning*. To put it plainly, "The Bible is not a book of hidden ideas demanding that the reader reinterpret the words to discover...

religious thoughts."[11] In other words, we want to just let the text say what it says, and not try to force it to say whatever we want it to say—no-matter how noble that want may be. Again, this all boils back down to the fact that God chose to communicate through specific people in a specific place and of a specific time to address specific issues. When we stray away from those specifics, the words lose their meaning. When this happens, even if we are using the same words, making them mean different things means that we are not getting the message God intended for us...this also means we are not getting a teaching that carries the authority of God's word. In short, when we do this, we may as well just turn on the television for our instruction because any meaning other than the intended meaning is just as fictitious as your favorite sitcom.

At first, it may seem a little lackluster that the Bible simply means what it means and we don't have the authority to just take it for whatever we fancy it to mean. However, if this is what you want to do, then why even bother with the Bible in the first place? There is no greater shame than having direct communication from God and ignoring it for our own ideas because there is no greater treasure aside from God himself, the Lord Jesus Christ, than his word to us. Therefore, let it be what it is. If it is challenging, let it be challenging; be challenged by it! Let God use it to grow you, stretch you, change you, and make you better. We can do this by safeguarding our interpretation, by following these basic rules, and, therefore, by letting God speak to us as he intended to.

Generalization—What is the Central Idea?

Observation and interpretation are the fundamentals for understanding what took place in the then and there of biblical history. In these stages we asked, "What does it say," and, "What does it mean?" This next phase of the process is sort of the bridging phase. With generalization, we ask, "What is the central idea?" In other words, we want to take the specific and detailed events that took place in literal history, and we want to pull from that what the big, general, or central idea was. This is a major principle of effective communication, as Richards and Bredfeldt put it, saying, "Whether we are considering a term paper, a speech, a sermon, or the word of God, it is essential to identify the author's thematic focus."[12]

I find it is often overlooked that that the authors in fact had a, or several focus points of their writings. The overlooking is particularly prevalent when we pluck little verses out for single serving usages, such as, "I can do all things through Christ who strengthens me," or "I am fearfully and wonderfully made." Those are great verses, and great things to ponder on, but they were said in a context of which the author had a primary focus or point to saying them. If we miss this point, then when we move from interpretation to application, we run the risk of missing the message all together. So, what we want to be able to do is sum up the prime point of a passage in one sentence. This might be a little difficult sometimes, especially with some of the more complex topics, or with larger sections of Scripture. There are, however, two questions we can ask that will help us narrow down our focus to the author's main point. First, we want to ask what the author is talking about. Then we want to ask what the author is saying about what they are talking about.[13]

We need to remember that the person writing already knew what they wanted to say. Sometimes we can overlook this because we tend to read in real time, as if we are getting play-by-play notes jotted down on the go by each author; this couldn't be further from the truth. Whether a prophet like Isaiah, an evangelist like John, or a pastor like Paul, each writer put careful thought and organization into their writings. When we remember this, that they all already knew exactly what they wanted to say, then it becomes easier for us to find that main idea from each piece of the writings, and for the writings as a whole as well. And the most beautiful part is that it is as easy as answering two questions; what is the author talking about, and what is the author saying about what they are talking about? "By answering both questions, the Bible student can begin to formulate a single sentence that entails the major idea or principle being taught in the passage."[14] Once this step is complete, and we have taken ahold of what might be called the *exegetical idea*, then we are ready to move on to the next phase.

Application—How Does This Apply to Me?

Having crossed the bridge of the exegetical idea, we are finally ready answer *here and now* questions. We are ready to begin to see how these various passages apply to each of our lives. Now, it is important to note that not every passage will apply to every situation at every time of a person's life. Figuring this out is extremely important; we must learn when to say, "This isn't for me right now." That being said, this is the stage of Bible study where God's word intimately intertwines with our lives. Sometimes it might be hard to imagine how the events happening in the lives of people so far removed from us can have an impact on our modern lives, but truly, "People in all periods of human history have lost loved ones, seen personal calamity, experienced hurt and broken relationships, and sought meaning to life."[15] These are the ties that bind us in the human experience, and God speaks to all of them through his interactions with mankind as they are recorded in the Scripture. It is this very "commonality in our lives that gives the Bible its timeless quality in application."[16]

Because there is only one proper interpretation of a given passage, but many applications, we must have some insight during the application process so that we do not step out of the bounds set by the interpretation. To put it plainly, the proper application will never contradict the proper interpretation. Since the proper interpretation falls under the rule of continuity in that no passage of Scripture can contradict the overall teaching of Scripture, so must no application go against the overall teaching of Scripture. This means no application of a passage should, for instance, lead one into sin of any kind. If your application of a passage somehow is leading you towards a romantic affair with a co-worker or friend, then you are not under God's authority; you are misinterpreting something along the way and/or misapplying it.

Much like everything else, then, we need to ask certain questions in order to keep us on the right track. Am I reading this as God intended it to be read, is there some sort of teaching or principle here that I can follow or learn, or is there a reprimand or rule to be corrected by? All of these questions fall in line with 2 Timothy 3:16, and ultimately leads to one meta-question, "In what way does this passage train us to be righteous?"[17] When these questions are answered, we might find that depending on our situation or need, there could be a different specific at times, or between our application and that of another person's, but if the process is followed properly, our applications and others' applications will always fall in line with the main bridging principle.

Implementation—What Will I Do?

All of this has been great so far, but honestly, how much is it really worth if it does not lead to anything? That is why there is one more phase of the five-part inductive study process—implementation. This is where we, quite literally, implement our application. You would think that this is a given part of the application process, but you might be surprised how many times application is discussed in Bible studies, church services, and small groups, only to have the people returning to their routines and doing nothing to actually *apply* the *application*. This is the reason for the implementation phase.

We want to be intentional with how God's word integrates with our daily living. Notice how the book of James says, "Be ye doers of the word, and not hearers only, deceiving your own selves (KJV)."[18] James is essentially saying that if we are not implementing God's word in our lives we are deceiving ourselves. So let's implement some of what we have learned so far and look at James's words in a larger portion, in order to gain a better idea of the context from which he makes his point—as we have discussed before. He says, "Understand this, my dear brothers and sisters: You must all be quick to listen, slow to speak, and slow to get angry. Human anger does not produce the righteousness God desires. So get rid of all the filth and evil in your lives, and humbly accept the words God has planted in your hearts, for it has the power to save your souls (NLT)."[19] Now, as a follow up to that statement, he continues with the first verse we read. Let's read it again, but this time in a more modern translation. Starting back at James 1:21, "So get rid of all the filth and evil in your lives, and humbly accept the word God has planted in your hearts, for it has the power to save your souls. But don't just listen to God's word. You must do what it says. Otherwise, you are only fooling yourselves (NLT)."[20]

God never intended the Scriptures to be entertainment. That's not to say that Bible study and church services have to be boring and lifeless, but I am simply saying that God's word is powerful, and it is intended to change our lives by leading us closer and closer to source of that power, God the Father and the Lord Jesus Christ. Now there are all kinds of things one can do to help them be intentional with their study, and these things will vary for people in different situations, and who are working on growing in different areas, but the one blanket principle is response. "We cannot study the God of the Bible through the pages of the Bible without response."[21] And when we do read it without responding, as James notes, we deceive ourselves into thinking any kind of progress has been made in our lives or in our relationship with God.

What, then, is the biggest response one can have? I think it is prayer. Think about what James said, "Get rid of the filth and evil in your lives…and be doers of God's word." How can we do this? After all, if it were that easy, wouldn't we all have done that already? The answer is that we cannot. We cannot do what it takes to live a godly life apart from God. This is why prayer should be our number one response. When we are having our devotional reading times, when we are doing an inductive study exercise and have arrived at some good application points, when we are feeling particularly convicted by something the pastor or preacher says in their sermon, we need to go straight to God with that.

I will give you one example from my own life of what this looks like before wrapping up this topic. When I became a Christian, and I was doing Bible study several times a week as well as thinking about joining a serve team at my church, I was still smoking pot. I kind of talked myself into thinking it was like spiritual and all that kind of stuff. However, I had come across some verses about being sober of mind. So I was beginning to feel a little convicted.

Left to my own devices, and even after discussion with some other Christians, I was able to justify my marijuana use, but my personal justification was not erasing the conviction I felt. Now, the point of this story, to be clear, is not to share my testimony and position on marijuana use, it is about Bible study.

In studying the Bible, I came across portions that seemed to contradict what I was doing with my life, and since "our goal [in Bible study] is to develop within ourselves the mind and heart of God,"[22] then the only appropriate response to study is to approach the very God whose mind and heart we are after. So, very simply, I went to God, and I asked him if he wanted me to make a change. I said, "If you show me that you don't want me to be doing this, then I will give it over to you." After this prayer, almost instantly God began to flood my heart and my mind with his reasons for wanting to change this specific behavior in my life. It was so much that I could not deny it, and I could not justify my behavior anymore, so I submitted and surrendered to God's will. I gave my behavior to him and told him to do with me as he saw fit. And he did just that. After almost twenty years of marijuana use, through Bible study and prayer, I responded to God's call for me to change. I implemented the general idea of a sober mind, which applied to my pot smoking, by going to God and giving him control over my personal freedom to use marijuana.

Conclusion

When we make coming to the Bible a priority in the same sense that premodern townsfolk would prioritize going to the well for their daily needs, then we can instantly appreciate a process by which we would draw water from the well, transport it to our place of living for application, and implement its use in our lives. In Bible study, we have this laid out for us in the five-part inductive study process. And when we honor the process, when we observe, interpret, generalize, apply, and implement God's word in our daily living, then we see, almost invariably, that God truly does have the power to change our lives.

Let us not miss the prime point, then, that our study in God's word should always lead us to God. He *is* speaking to us through his recorded interactions with humanity as they are presented in the pages of the Bible... Since this intentional revelation is God speaking to the world; we must respond! If we do not respond, if we simply let God's voice fade off into the distance, there will be no growth, no change, and no communion with God.

AFTERWORD

Studying in and about God's word is nothing short of amazing, truly. It might be hard to imagine that being the case at first, but the more you dig, the more you learn, the more you grow, and the more you crave more. I can remember before I became a Christian, I would tell lies about the Bible—the most primary lie being that I had actually read the Bible. I didn't! This is how I know a lot of people out there now claiming to have read it are lying. So, it is interesting also that I would repeat things like, "The Bible is full of errors and contradictions," or, "The Bible is just a book of myths and fairy tales."

Why is this so interesting? Because I was lying! I had no idea what I was talking about because I had never really read it or studied it. I had no clue what it was about or what was contained within its pages. Now, fast forward a short few years, and I know the Bible to be the best, most truthful, and most valuable piece of literature known to man. I have over seven hundred books in my library, and none of them come close to being as valuable as the Bible.

That is why it has truly been an honor and a pleasure to put this work together about some of the basic fundamentals concerning the Bible. And I don't begin to fool myself with thinking that this work is anything more than that. While I learned so much in my writing of and research for this book, I know that I only scratched the surface for you all reading it. I know this because of the numerous books I read to gather my material—numerous books that went so much deeper than I did, and yet only scratched the surface themselves. This is why I encourage you to investigate my sources. When I first read *The Case for Christ*, by Lee Strobel, I knew he had only glanced the tip of the iceberg. So, I did exactly what I am advising you to do; I went out and I got as much literature as I could by the experts that he interviewed so that I could go deeper. Do this! You will not regret it.

Just the Beginning

Apart from me simply scratching the surface on the topic of the Bible, I am also just getting started on the topic of basic Christian essentials. What I mean is that this book is just meant to be a first volume in a set of several. I struggled whether to write about prayer or Bible study because they are both essential, and I only decided to go with Bible study first because it is actually the Bible that should be our primary source about learning to pray. That being said, they should really go hand in hand.

So, as I continue my journey as a minister, an author, a scholar, and a teacher, prayer is the next topic I wish to tackle. As I said before, Bible study should always lead us to respond to God. That response needs to begin with prayer. So, while I pray this volume has helped you get started, my prayer is also that the next volume will take us even deeper. There is always so much more to learn, and so much closer to get with God. Even though he indwells us, even though he is everywhere all the time, even though he never leaves us nor forsakes us, there is always more of himself he wants to reveal. So keep digging, keep searching, and keep reading; those who seek and keep seeking will find.

Some Additions

Before we end here, now that I've commented on where we just came from and where I want to go next, I thought it would be nice to include a couple of my academic works that might help fill out any holes left behind, or answer any questions I may have left unanswered. Not that I think I have all the answers, but God has definitely blessed me with being able to study him, his word, and his creation, so I seek to include as much of that as I can in my presentations to you.

That said, these other works will be a bit more academic than any of the previous chapters, and will at times be repeating information already touched upon. But I hope you can enjoy them nonetheless. Sometimes I wonder what all my learning, research, and writing is all for, and apart from the simple fact that it is all ultimately for God as something I believe he has called me to, I know that it is at the very least for the purpose of sharing. So, may God bless you with what he has so richly blessed me with.

Final Words

From here, there really isn't too much more to say. Thank you so much for sticking with me to the end. It really has been an honor and a pleasure. I hope this book has sparked some deep curiosity, answered some good questions, and caused some interesting conversations for you. But above all, I hope it has helped you draw nearer to God. In any event, whatever any of it has done for you… To God be the glory, in Jesus name. Amen!

APPENDIX 1

Introduction

This first piece is an extension on the topic of the inspiration of Scripture. It was originally written for a course called *Introduction to Christian History and Thought*, at Regent University, and it seeks to explain some the alternative views concerning the inspiration of Scripture. It is a short work, but I am including it because I feel it will compliment well the previous discussion on the inerrancy of the Scripture since this book's treatment of the topic did not delve very deeply into the alternative views. It is always good to be aware of what the other popular thoughts on a topic are.

Inspired and Authentic:
Theologies of the Modern Era and Their View on Scripture

The Bible remains the topic of unending discussion, debates, and disputes among people of all social classes and ethnicity. The rich and the poor, the highly educated and the not so highly educated, Americans and Asians and Africans alike; everyone, for better or for worse, is obligated to make a judgment on the Bible—perhaps more so than any other literary work in existence. At the top of the list of decisions to make regarding the Bible are the issues of errancy, fallibility, and inspiration.

Traditionally, it is believed that the Bible is the inerrant, infallible, and inspired word of God. However, traditions have a somewhat unstable place in this post-enlightenment, postmodern era of humanity. Many claim that truth must trump tradition, and that we can know the truth apart from any so-called divine revelation. Of course, it should be noted, that the Bible itself is the very source of the traditional truth claim that it is God's inerrant, self-revelation. "Scripture presents God's truth as revealed, objective, absolute, universal, eternally engaging, antithetical, systematic and an end in itself."[1] Given the validity of this truth, "There is no reason for theology to alter or adjust this understanding of truth when it comes to Scripture as God's revelation or with respect to the formulations of theological systems."[2] But this is precisely what has happened in the wake of the reformation and enlightenment era.

In an effort to remain "relevant" in the presence of the self-proclaimed master worldview of the modern universe, scientism, Christianity has struggled against itself for a place of significance. This resulting in many schisms, evolutions, and systematic renovations to Christian theology. At the center of all these theological shifts, is, as noted earlier, the traditionally held belief that the Bible is the inerrant and infallible, inspired word of God. Many of the schools of thought on theology examined in this work have completely abandoned this biblically proclaimed truth, while others have sought to side step it in crafty yet casual manners. How unfortunate for them and for humanity. Perhaps "The greatest problem with human reasoning occurs when it vainly attempts to become autonomous of God and divine revelation."[3] This is, nevertheless, the course humanity has widely chosen.

Despite this, there remains at least one theological division true and faithful to the right view of Scripture—the historic, orthodox, evangelical view. Before discussing this view, a look at the contemporary views of Liberal, Neo-Orthodox, Extreme Fundamental, and Neo-Evangelicalism, with particular regard to their common view of Scripture, will help appropriate the proposition that the middle way, historic, orthodox, Evangelical view of Scripture is superior in all ways for both life and activity within the church, and within and throughout society.

Liberalism and the Freedom to Choose

"'Liberal' as a self-commending description, implying readiness to welcome new ideas and freedom from the restraint obscurantist traditionalism, and irrational bigotry, has been adopted at various times over the past 150 years."[4] Germane to this work are, "Protestants world-wide who held post-enlightenment views stemming from Schleiermacher and Ritschl in theology, Kant and Hegel in philosophy, and Strauss and Julius Wellhausen in biblical study."[5] It is also important to note the distinction between doctrinal liberalism, and liberalism in biblical scholarship. "The former was an undermining or denial of the traditional doctrines of the Christian faith, while the latter challenged the authenticity, historicity and divine inspiration of the Bible."[6]

Christian liberalism, in a positive note, was asking if they could, "Preach the old, old story in a new, new world in which the way of thinking was supposedly more sophisticated than in the early, medieval or reformation worlds?"[7] Before long, however, confidence in mankind's newfound autonomy demanded that it was Christianity which had to assimilate to modern thought, and not the other way around.[8]

A nearly universally agreed upon point in liberalism was the desire to break away from Scripture as the ultimate authority. "Reason, culture, experience and science would all be employed in challenge to the classical authority of revelation."[9] This end result can easily be traced back to the roots of the movement. Namely, that, "Schleiermacher reduced Christianity to a single aspect: The romantic notion of feeling."[10] He writes, "I ask therefore, that you turn from everything usually reckoned religion, and fix your regard on the inward emotions and dispositions, as all utterances and acts of inspired men direct."[11] Thus, the Bible, "Became treated as a record of human religious experience rather than a revelation from God or a record of God's act in history."[12]

From this foundation, David Strauss, regarding the Gospels, "Contended that the four evangelists had actually fabricated what they wrote and that Jesus was a deceiver and an imposter."[13] Elizabeth Cady Stanton, "Interprets the creation of male and female in the image of God to imply, [...] That we have a 'Heavenly Mother' as well as a 'Heavenly Father.'"[14] Bultmann feels that, "Modern man' cannot accept the New Testament message because he cannot accept the mythical worldview."[15] And, finally, John Hick feels that, "All different religions can have their slots in the broadcasting schedule and have their say—so long as they don't suggest that anyone else is wrong or make any ultimate truth claims."[16]

Liberalism, despite itself, had some positive contributions, such as its emphasis on the human element of Scripture, the focus on matters of higher criticism, and the emphasis on the need for biblical scholarship,[17] but there is much wrong with the Liberal position. Liberalism's belief is contrary to the claims of the Bible in that, "The Bible claims that the very words of Scripture comprise the unbreakable, indestructible, ultimately authoritative, and absolutely true word of God."[18] It is also contrary to the teachings of Christ. "Jesus taught that the Bible is the divinely inspired and authoritative word of God."[19] So, "How can Liberals be followers of the teachings of Jesus if they deny one of the essential teachings of Jesus, namely, that the Bible is God's word?"[20] Finally, aside from the fact that Liberalism is based on unjustified antisupernaturalism,[21] it is also inconsistent with its own assumptions, "For it uses the Bible as an authentic basis for determining what the Spirit of Jesus is and then in turn uses the Spirit of Jesus to attack the authenticity of large parts of the Bible."[22] In the end, having dispensed with the authority of Scripture, Liberalism replaces it with the individuals feeling and experience. In this way, Liberal theology may still use the Bible, but not be bound by it.

From the Rubble Rebuild: Neo-Orthodoxy

A particularly glaring flaw in Liberalism was its view of sin, or rather the lack thereof. For the Liberal, there was no sin, only ignorance. Then came the First World War. "The evil which was laid bare struck a mortal blow against the old Liberal idea that evil was only ignorance which might be corrected by education."[23] The free morality mentality of Liberalism was volatile, and the need for a structured Christianity was clear. Not willing to return to the old system, however, these liberally thinking non-liberals built something new—a Neo-Orthodoxy.

"Karl Barth became the leader of the Neo-Orthodox (not his term) reaction to nineteenth-century Liberalism,"[24] but his thoughts and views were in many ways a continuation of the ideas set forth earlier by P.T. Forsyth, and Soren Kierkegaard. In Kierkegaard, truth lies in subjectivity,[25] so it follows that in Forsyth, "Authority in Christian theology lies in the Gospel, which is recorded in the Bible, rather than the Bible itself as a book."[26] All this leading up to Barth and the Neo-Orthodox view on God and Scripture that, "God is the wholly other."[27] Or in other words, God is truly unknowable. In a redefinition of terms, Barth claims that theology is to be found in God's word, only God's word isn't necessarily the Bible. "The written word of Scripture and the proclaimed word are not themselves revelation, but they are fallible human words pointing to God's revelation,"[28] as Barth taught. "They become God's word when he chooses to speak through them."[29]

Foreword from Barth, others contribute to Neo-Orthodox development. These include Dietrich Bonhoeffer, who insists that, "Christians must learn to speak of God in a secular way and to live their Christianity in a secular way."[30] Wolfhart Pannenberg, who, opposed to Barth, "insists that the truth claims of Christianity, and the historicity of the resurrection in particular, are open to verification,"[31] And, Finally, Reinhold Niebuhr, who viewed Scripture as something to be symbolized into palatable yet teachable means; "The idea of the resurrection of the body is a Biblical symbol in which modern minds take the greatest offense and which has long since been displaced in most modern versions of Christian faith by the idea of the immortality of the soul."[32]

Neo-Orthodox theology placed a healthy emphasis on the centrality of Christ and rejection of Bibliolatry (The worship of the Bible), as well as "On the need for a personal, existential encounter with God."[33] However, the Neo-Orthodox view of Scripture, like Liberalism's view, is biblically unfounded.[34] "It is contrary to what the Bible claims for itself, that it is the verbal, plenary Word of God."[35] It is also an interesting inconsistency to say that "God can act in human history but he cannot speak in human language,"[36] which Neo-Orthodoxy does say. To this one must ask if God created humanity with a language God does not speak?[37] "Indeed, it is a denial of the principle of analogy to claim that God can give perfections he does not have."[38]

Aside from being Christologically incoherent, the Neo-Orthodox view of Scripture is practically unfruitful.[39] "While the Neo-Orthodox view sounds better than the Liberal view, it reduces to the same factual flaw: that the Bible is not the infallible word of God but only the fallible words of men about God."[40] When considering this view, and trying to fit the Christian salvation into it, one must ask, "How can one trust his eternal destiny to fallible human teaching known to be riddled with errors?"[41]

Middle Way Evangelicalism

A large cause of these erroneous theological perspectives, at least as far as America is concerned, was an "influx of immigrants," who brought a "plurality of religious beliefs and subcultures."[42] Combined with that fact, "The rise of the theory of evolution had made it popular to question the existence of a personal God as the sole creator of life."[43] Despite all that, "Evangelicals have, to a greater or lesser extent, sought to adapt to the modern world. But they have insisted that this process should not lead to the distortion of the biblical Gospel."[44]

Evangelicals from a variety of backgrounds joined to preserve the basic truths of Protestant Christianity.[45] "Their rallying point was the inspiration and infallibility of Scripture—which seemed as a touchstone for orthodoxy as it was a doctrine which united the movement against Liberalism, and which could fairly be held to undergird the other elements of orthodox Protestantism."[46] However, proper Evangelicalism is a middle way between the two incorrect extremes of Neo-Evangelicalism, and Extreme Fundamentalism.[47]

Fundamentalism, Neo-Evangelicalism, and Evangelicalism in Contrast

A proper, orthodox view of Scripture as the inspired word of God is similar to the proper, orthodox view of the deity and humanity of Jesus Christ. Much like how Christ is fully God and fully man, "So also the Bible is fully God's word and also fully the words of its human authors."[48] Extreme Fundamentalists are guilty of biblical Docetism, that is, diminishing its human side. This is done when they fail to take seriously the many (non-fallacious) human aspects of the Bible, including culture, literary genre, and human interests.[49]

On the other end, the Neo-Evangelicals "wish to maintain the inspiration and authority of Scripture...Wish it to be the final norm for faith...And wouldn't feel free to criticize its theology— but do not feel that this need exclude factual errors in the Bible in the areas of history or geography, say."[50] However, this simply cannot be true. If the Bible is God's word, "every truth claim it makes is factually accurate."[51] Otherwise, it cannot be God's word. When all is said and done, "The Neo-Evangelical view of the Bible is not better than the Liberal view, the Neo-Evangelical just makes it seem better."[52]

A Final Look at Evangelical Christianity

Between the extremes of all the other views mentioned above, "Is the historic, orthodox, evangelical view that affirms both the full divinity and full humanity of Scripture in concurrence with the words of God and the words of the human authors he moved upon to produce a God-breathed product."[53] This view is held by Christians who, "Are both backward-looking and forward-looking people, a people with historical discretion and confident expectation."[54] The truly orthodox Evangelical has nothing to hide and nothing to fear about their belief and faith in the inspiration of Scripture, and is not ashamed in any way—nor will they allow themselves to be. In this sense, they are forthright and confident about their faith, and are willing to lay it all out on display in a way uncharacteristic of any of the aforementioned, unorthodox groups or systems. By this I refer to things such as the International Council on Biblical Inerrancy, who are willing to draft both brief and expanded statements of belief, in the spirit of full disclosure.[55]

The best expression of the sound Evangelical view on the inspiration of Scripture, is perhaps that of the Old Princetonian, Benjamin Breckenridge Warfield, who's idea is captured in this following paragraph.

> The Human writers wrote freely—but they were prepared for their task by God and he revealed himself to them to the extent that was necessary for their task. 'If God wished to give his people a series of letters like Paul's, he prepared a Paul to write them—and the Paul he brought to the task was a Paul who spontaneously would write just such letters.' The result is that the writers wrote precisely what God wanted. Thus one can talk of

'verbal inspiration', or the inspiration of the very words of the text—in opposition to the idea that God merely put ideas into the minds of the writers and left them to get on with the task of writing them down as best they could. Because the writers wrote precisely what God wanted, the message of the Bible is his message and the Bible can be called his word. It follows therefore that what the Bible teaches is true.[56]

Conclusion

It is no doubt clear that I write from a historical, orthodox, Evangelical Christian world-view. However, one must not suppose that this has made me victim to bias in my position. Having examined the various writings and evidences pertaining to each theological view presented in this work, I have no other choice but to proclaim that the middle way Evangelical view of Scripture is superior to the others. Or, perhaps Schleiermacher was right when he says, "Every Christian, before he enters at all upon inquiries of this kind, has already the inward certainty that his religion cannot take any other form."[57] Whatever the case with that may be, with regards to what is best for congregational/church-life, and what is best for integration and participation in society, the inerrant, infallible, inspired word of God, view of Scripture, which is best put forth by orthodox Evangelical Christians, is superior in all facets and functions.

A big danger of the other views is that there is no accountability. The view that makes emotional experience the ultimate authority is subject to the whimsical and fickle tendencies of emotions. In this sense, where the Scripture says, "But I say to you that everyone who looks at a woman with lust for her has already committed adultery with her in his heart (NASB)."[58] If that is not the real and true word of God, then really and truly, who cares? And what if the stakes are higher? Many Liberal and Neo-Orthodox views were developed over a dislike of the doctrine of Hell, but if the Bible is just fallible words of men, if one doesn't like something, it is okay to explain it away or disregard it altogether.

However, when the Bible is the infallible, inerrant, inspired Word of God, then any who believe that must strive to obey its commands, and follow in the footsteps of the Lord Jesus Christ. Footsteps of submission, of humility, and yes, occasional righteous indignation. But this means loving the brothers and sisters of the congregation, and respecting the authorities of the world. It also means holding those in theological authority (i.e. pastors, deacons, presbyters, and so on) to the standard rule of ultimate theological authority, the Bible—the Word of God. It means engaging with the culture, and adhering to all possible laws of the land. It means all this and so much more, but it only means any of these things as the inspired word of God. Otherwise, the Bible is simply meaningless, and we should, in the words of David Hume, "Commit it then to the flames, for it can contain nothing but sophistry and illusion."[59]

APPENDIX 2

Introduction

This paper was written for *Systematic Theology I*, at Regent University. It attempts to explain why Scripture carries the authority of being God's words, and how to properly read it and study it in a manner that allows it to retain that authority from God. I am including this work as an extension and compliment to chapter 7, *Coming to the Well*, as well as chapter 5, *The Pure Waters of God*. It is my hope that this paper can satisfy anything left lacking in those two areas of discussion.

The Authority of Scripture: Truth, Revelation, and Proper Interpretation

The Bible being God breathed (theopneustos) means that it contains God's words to humanity exactly as he wanted them spoken, even though God chose to speak these words through men who wrote of their own free wills to address specific situations of specific peoples in specific times, places, and cultures. Therefore, it is the contention—and thesis—of this work that the Bible and the lessons taught from it only retain their quality of God-breathed authority insofar as they are translated, read, and taught from in accordance with the original intended message that God inspired.

Otherwise, if one does not present what the original authors were inspired to communicate, they present their own ideas, their own messages, and their own teachings which do not carry the weight and authority of God-breathed (theopneustos) Scripture.

This proposition pulls from three points leading up to, and an inference drawn from the doctrines of the inspiration of Scripture; that is, specifically, that the Bible is God's authoritative word. The first task is to establish the existence of truth. The second task is establishing the writings collected in the Bible as truthful presentations of events (insofar as each individual piece of literature claims to be), or as truthful representations of situations the authors themselves were engaged in. The third task is to argue these truthful records of real events as the truthful records of the events by which God reveals himself to humanity. These three tasks are points leading up to the doctrine of inspiration. From these points, a clear inference is drawn: insofar as the writings of Scripture capture real events in real space and in real time, that also are the records of God's self-revelation to humanity, they must be interpreted, read, and taught from in a literal-historical fashion— that is, they only hold the authority of God's self-revelation if they are read and taught from as the original authors intended them to be understood.

Establishing the Existence of Truth

"For this I have come into the world," Jesus says when questioned by Pontius Pilate, "to testify to the truth (NASB)."[1] But what is Jesus saying? Does he mean his truth, Pilate's truth, the Christian truth, Jewish truth, or maybe the Roman's truth? Perhaps this is Pilate's sentiment in the next verse where "Pilate said to Him, 'What is truth (NASB)?"[2] It is likely not the case, however, that Pilate was having a moment of philosophical reflection; he was more likely frustrated with the situation and his inability to threaten what he would have considered a straight answer from Jesus.[3] It is perhaps possible, though, that, while not questioning the nature of truth, Pilate was questioning the validity of it. As is if to say, "What difference does it make if you are innocent or not?" Or, more generally, does it matter what the truth is?

Now, consider why a person might wonder if Pilate was philosophically questioning the nature of truth—whether it is objective or subjective, knowable or unknowable, or relative? The answer is because these questions are philosophically relevant today. But while it is true they are questions being asked in the 21st century...were they questions Pilate would have asked in the context of his interviewing Jesus? This is important, and it is a prime focus of the main thesis of this work, but it is only highly important insofar as there is such a thing as objective truth. Since this is a topic of today's world, then, it must be addressed because it applies directly to not only the value of the Scriptures themselves, but also in how one interprets them. So, it is asked here, does truth exist, and if so what is it?

Truth Through the Ages: How Do We Know?

The Bible, as a whole, makes many distinctions and contrasts between that which is true and that which is error, and more specifically to this discussion, "John's understanding of truth presupposes a correspondence view of truth."[4] This means that when Jesus says to Pilate that he was born to testify the truth, he was vouching for that which corresponds to reality. To Jesus, to John, and to his intended readers, there is an ultimate reality for which what is true conforms to over that which is deceitful or in error contradicts.[5] But how does one know? There are many statements being made about realty, so how can one know which ones are true, if there even is such a thing, if they are opposing statements about reality?

These are not new thoughts. As far back as Plato, thinkers have been trying to work out what it means to "know" something.[6] Interestingly enough, however, truth has always been a condition of propositional knowledge, "and the traditional or standard definition of propositional knowledge is the view that knowledge is justified true belief."[7] So, again, one gets stuck. If truth is that which corresponds to reality, but to know about reality one must be able to distinguish truth, how can one know what is true? As a very broad answer, there have been, or are, three general means of knowing truth. First is revelation, then reason and research, and finally, relativity.

Revelation, Research and Reason, and Relativity

When Jesus said he came to bear witness to the truth, he meant that his life was a testimony of the truthfulness of God's revelation. In this view, the revelation mode, "truth comes from the disclosure of a personal and moral God who makes himself known."[8] It is important to understand the implication of this. "The claim that God has revealed himself to us presupposes objective truth as the cognitive content of revelation…truth that is not dependent on any creature's subjective feelings, desires or beliefs."[9] In other words, truth in this mode is obtained directly from the source, God— through Scripture. This mode became particularly prevalent after the advent of Christ, which would be expected if he actually was the evidence of God's reliability concerning truth.

The next mean is research and reason. This is an observational and empirical approach—basically scientific. This mean is associated with modernism and the enlightenment, and is generally thought to begin between the sixteen and seventeen-hundreds. As a broad capture, "The modernist vision presupposed the power of rationality to discover objective truth. They desired a rational, scientific worldview over the perceived irrationality and acrimony stemming from religion, and the possibility of progress through humanity's emancipation from received dogma and superstition."[10] This mode of thought still admits there is an objective truth, truth apart from whatever one might think, believe, or feel, but they believe the only way to become aware of this truth is through observation of measurable phenomena. In other words, if it cannot be seen, smelled, touched, tasted, or heard, or somehow measured otherwise, it is not truth or cannot be known (So no revelation, i.e. no Scripture).

Finally, there is relativity. This is essentially associated with postmodernism, which is very much so a dominating philosophy of current times. In this mode of thinking, there is no such thing as objective truth, and if there were, for various reasons, one would never be able to know what it was. The means for finding truth here is subjective. It is communal, relative, and relational. This is the mindset that says, "What is true for me may not be true for you." Interestingly enough, this worldview "ends up being more of a preference or prejudice than a philosophically argued position in the classical sense, given the postmodernist disparaging of reason as a way to ascertain objective reality."[11]

Considering these three modes of truth, it may be surprising to some that the only one of these three categories operating on a sufficiently high plain, encompassing the most aspects of known reality, is the first—revelation. The second, reason and research, is absolutely right that scientific investigation is a good means to gain truthful knowledge; it falls into the realm of error, however, when it is claimed to be the only means. Then there is relativity. It is often overlooked that culture and relationship certainly can reveal truth that may otherwise be hard to discover. It is also right that the subjective experience plays an important role in finding truth; it is wrong, however, when taken to the degree that says, "There is no knowable truth beyond the subjective." All things considered, then, revelation, offers the best possible picture of reality because it includes the observable and measurable material world, and it includes the subjective experience in the process, whereas either of these other means excludes one of the other important component to knowing truth.

Skepticism and Rebellion

Many would say the heart of the issue with truth is skepticism, and to a degree this is true. The modern age expressed skepticism that truth could be established through revelation, and the postmodern thinking was skeptical that truth even existed or that it was knowable. The former is a sort of limited or mitigated skepticism where certain things can absolutely be known by observation and reason, but things such as metaphysical or theological propositions cannot be known (because they cannot be observed and measured).[12] The latter would be a thoroughgoing or complete skepticism—nothing is true and if it is, one still cannot know for sure; the best one might have is a strong belief. To this brand, Geisler and Feinberg observe, "At first, arguing with a skeptic can be an invigorating experience. But ultimately it becomes frustrating, for a good skeptic is prevented from ever agreeing on any premise, making it impossible for the argument to even get started."[13] In other words, if pressed the complete skeptic merely has to assert that there is no premise one can truly be sure of. Therefore, the skeptic is free from the responsibility of defending their position.

The obvious flaw of the complete skepticism/subjective truth model is that the very model itself makes ultimate claims about reality, or, in other words, claims of objective truth. "The skeptic's assertion that we cannot know anything is itself a claim about knowledge. If the skeptic's claim is false, then we need not worry about the skeptic's charge. On the other hand, if it is true, then his position is self-contradictory, because we know at least one thing—that we cannot know anything."[14] The strongest practical evidence against skepticism, however, is application. In everyday life, skepticism simply fails; it is inapplicable to the human experience. "Imagine the skeptic coming to the railroad crossing… and asking himself if the world is real and if that is a real train thundering down the track? Hardly! He stops and waits just like the rest of us."[15] On the deepest and most basic level of human thought, one is aware of the reality, of the truth, regarding their existence.

The real issue, then, is not skepticism; it is desire, and it is rebellion. The enlightenment era did not seek to do away with revelation as a means of knowing truth because they thought it was a faulty means, but more so because they did not agree with the propositions. The notion of sins and obedience, penalty and punishment, these go against the human desire for autonomous existence. So, the limited skeptic decides these undesirable notions are not necessarily affirmed if the means of knowing them is denied.

Not to be outdone, or as if rebellion is addictive to the collective human consciousness, empirical objectivity is next to be rejected by the following generation of skepticism—postmodernism. "Science is deemed domineering and oppressive and unable to discern objective truth, and 'progress' only describes whatever serves the interests and ideologies of the dominant culture."[16] In the end, it is reality that is domineering and oppressive to ones who wish to have complete control, so reality is systematically and progressively denied, but reality cannot be completely denied since that which exists is hopelessly bound to the conditions of existence as the canvas of reality, so it always becomes the previous definition of reality to stand trial in a current philosophy's attempt of emancipation—whatever that previous definition may have been.

Assuming, then, the relative thinker, the skeptic or postmoderner, has some concept that there is such a thing as reality, even they (even if unwittingly) believe their belief corresponds to what is real. If they think that truth is a subjective concept, they likely do not believe that truth is a subjective concept simply because this is what they think, or that it is true for some but for others objective truth might be real. Rather, they believe it is ultimately what the condition of reality is. This is where the real nature of truth, and the real proof of its existence, comes into play. If there is a God, if there is no God, if there are many gods, these things are either true or false. They are not, however, true or false because a person believes them; they are true or false because they either do or do not correspond with what the actual condition of reality is.

If a person claims there is a thousand dollars in their hand, it may be true; there may actually be a thousand dollars in their hand. However, if a person claims there is a thousand dollars in

162

their hand—even if they believe with all of their heart that there is a thousand dollars in their hand—it can be false. The thousand dollars either is in their hand or it isn't, and the fact of if it is or is not is independent of whether they believe it is or is not. This is a testable experiment that shows there is a reality apart from one's belief; an ultimate, independent, and objective reality. This realty should be sought at all times. One's beliefs should be measured, tried, and tested against it—not just because they were told, not simply regarding empirical data, and not solely based on subjective experience, but in consideration of all of these things. When held to this standard, a belief will stand or fall. It will prove to be true or false and whatever the outcome, the person holding the belief will be better in the end because "it is precisely belief in a truth beyond one's own thoughts and culture that allows one to be rebuffed and reconstructed by reality."[17]

Establishing the Writings of the Bible as Truthful Accounts of Actual Events

It may be tedious to discuss whether truth and knowledge are possible, but such is the condition of the time and culture in modern academics and philosophy. Moving forward from that, and having established truth as that which corresponds to reality, the next question is whether the Bible does or does not correspond to reality. Many people would simply declare something like, "The Bible is the Word of God and, therefore, it must be true because God cannot tell a lie or be in error." To this, those of a like mind might cheer, "Yea!" However, those who do not hold such a firm belief in the possibility of metaphysical reality would jeer, "Nay!" They would simply declare, contrary to the previous position,

"The Bible is nothing more than the words of men and, therefore, it must be false because humans can lie or be in error." Notice that both positions are making truth claims about reality. One says that the Bible corresponds to reality because it was given by God. The other says that it does not correspond to reality because it was written by men. So how does one go about engaging the topic on reasonable terms? The answer is to establish a common ground to start from on which both positions agree. The minimal place to begin, then, is that the Bible is nothing less than a book written by men.

From this universally agreeable position, one may quickly realize that the Bible is not even actually one book, but many; it is many individual works, some large and some small, written by many different men, accounting for the history of the church, back to the Jews, to the Israelites, and ultimately for humanity. So, the main question to be asked here is if these men who wrote the books accounting for the history of humanity through the ages and through multiple people groups were accurate. In other words, is what they wrote true? Does it correspond to reality? Now, again, there are two presuppositions which a majority of people take on this question. One is to say that they cannot be false because they were inspired by God, and the other is to say that they are sure to be false because they were written by men. It is the contention of this work, however, that both presuppositions be set aside for the time being.

If one is conducting honest inquiry, then letting go of presuppositions in light of the evidence is the only right thing to do. To service the skeptical person, it is only fair to set aside the notion, even if strongly believed, that God produced the Scriptures so they must be true; if this is, after all, the case, then the truth will stand on its own merit. To service the one who already trusts the Scriptures, the skeptic must admit that there are many works written by men which do not contain error. So, from baseline, it is best to simply assume nothing. With no presumptions, no presuppositions, and no preconceived notions, the question can honestly be asked, are the writings in the Bible truthful accounts of actual events?

When one sets aside any *a priori* judgments or conclusion, or even information, the only thing left is to go to the source of the topic. In other words, to set aside any error in interpretations, unfounded opinions, or the proverbial axe to grind, it is prudent to start at square one—the documents themselves. What does the Bible say? When looking at the actual texts, it becomes quickly apparent that the writings in the Bible declare or imply propositions. To go even further, however, beyond making truth claims, many writings explicitly claim to be telling the truth. One of the most compelling comes from the apostle Paul in a document written to the Corinthian Christians about midway through the first century AD. Paul writes,

> What I received I passed on to you as of first importance: that Christ died for our sins according to the Scriptures, that he was buried, that he was raised on the third day according to the Scriptures, and that he appeared to Cephas, and then to the Twelve. After that, he appeared to more than five hundred of the brothers and sisters at the same time, most of whom are still living, though some have fallen asleep. Then he appeared to James, then to all the apostles, and last of all he appeared to me also (NIV).[18]

Now, the topic of Paul's discussion is not the point of noting what he wrote. The point, rather, is that he is claiming to truthfully provide information that corresponds to reality. He says he is passing on what was passed on to him. He also claims that there are many eyewitnesses to corroborate the information he was giving. Finally, he claims to himself be an eyewitness to the subject matter of his discussion. Paul's prime intent here is to essentially say, "I am telling the truth!" This is not uncharacteristic of Paul. In his letter to the Christians in Rome, he explicitly says, "I speak the truth in Christ—I am not lying, my conscience confirms it through the Holy Spirit (NIV)."[19]

Paul is not the only New Testament author who declares his truthful accounts. Peter says, "I will always remind you of these things, even though you know them and are firmly established in the truth…For we did not follow cleverly devised stories when we told you about the coming of our Lord Jesus Christ in power, but we were eyewitnesses of his majesty (NIV)."[20] Peter also is essentially saying, "You know what we are saying is true, just as well as we know, since we were there." There are several more statements specifically claiming truthful accounts, but not to belabor the point, there is one more that will be presented here. The writer Luke, who is known as a physician, historian, and traveling companion of the apostle Paul, opens his two-volume work with a compelling statement. Luke writes,

> Many have undertaken to draw up an account of the things that have been fulfilled among us, just as they were handed down to us by those who from the first were eyewitnesses and servants of the word. With this in mind, since I myself have carefully investigated everything from the beginning, I too decided to write an orderly account for you…so that you may know the certainty of the things you have been taught (NIV).[21]

When it comes to Paul and Peter, they are fundamentally saying the same things, "We are telling the truth, and we have proof because we saw what we speak of and so did others, so if you doubt us you can investigate our claims." Luke's statement is different because he is essentially responding to that challenge, saying, "I was not there, but I was given an account by those who were there, so I carefully investigated what they said. Now, I am presenting you with my findings so you can be certain that what you were taught corresponds with reality—with what actually happened."

Verification

It is a strong place of start to understand that the Bible is not said to be true simply on assumption, but rather, that the individual writers of the documents claimed themselves to be giving truthful accounts of actual events. However, for many this is not good enough. After all, any person telling a lie wants their listener to believe they are telling the truth. What is necessary, then, is verification to justify the belief in the authors' claims. For Luke or his readers, or Paul and Peter and their readers, it was no terrible task to verify their claims because if they truly did correspond to reality then many people would be able to corroborate their claims—a point which is in fact a key part of their claims. For the modern reader, however, this is not so. There is nobody left in the market to give an accounting; there is not even a market left to visit. Since this is the case, now is the time in the investigation to turn to outside sources.

Ancient Sources

Several approaches are available, but when one is so far removed as the modern reader, it may be prudent to shoot for quality over quantity. In this sense, as far as outside ancient sources are concerned, it is of interest to consider what those who have no motivation to corroborate the accounts have to say. These are not highly detailed representations of vast amounts of information, but they do offer corroboration to fundamental details of the Bible—namely, details about Jesus Christ. Of first importance, consider two Jewish sources. There is an early account in the works of a Jewish historian, Josephus, and a later account in what is known as the Babylonian Talmud. Again, the specific details are somewhat limited, but, according to prominent professor of New Testament studies, Dr. Bruce Metzger, "In general, they confirm early Christian tradition by giving independent—and even hostile—testimony that Jesus of Nazareth really existed."[22] Metzger is being modest, which becomes apparent as he continues on, saying, "It is noteworthy also that the Talmud refers to Jesus' power to perform miracles…and to his claim to be the divine Son of God. The defamatory account of his birth seems [also] to reflect a knowledge of the Christian tradition that Jesus was born the son of the Virgin Mary."[23]

Metzger also speaks of three different Roman writers who corroborate to one degree or another the teachings of the Bible concerning Jesus. In summation, these sources (Pliny the Younger, Tacitus, and Suetonius) confirm "that he was a historical figure who lived in Palestine during the early years of the first century, that he gathered a group of followers about himself, and that he was condemned under Pontius Pilate."[24] Even though this seems like a scanty amount of information, what it does—between both

Jewish sources and all three Roman sources—is provide a concrete corroboration for the main topic for which the biblical writers claim to be speaking the truth about.

Having treated the hostile sources first, it is important to note that agreeance does not destroy the credibility of a source. The fact that the Jewish and Roman sources are anti-Christian in nature certainly lend credibility to their testimony, but the fact that early Christian sources agree with what the Bible says does not necessarily discredit their information…particularly if the reports of the biblical writers are true—as they claim to be. It should be noted that so many hundreds of years later, it is much more a matter of surface level faith than it would have been in the first and second century. This close to the actual events, the general population would have sharp objections to the writings if the facts they claim did not align with reality. When Paul and Peter claim to be eyewitnesses, and claim that there are hundreds of other eyewitnesses, they are subjecting themselves to the scrutiny of their readers. If they wrote false reports, their writings would have been known by many to be false, and they would have developed reputations as liars.

In this sense, they would have surely died out in popularity and reproduction. This, however, is not the case at all. What is seen is exactly the opposite. The writers of the biblical documents of the New Testament were so meticulously accurate and verifiable, that their reports reached mass production in a time where things simply were not mass produced. This is the case so much so to the point that long before the individual writings were collected and canonized into what is known now as the Bible, the writings were so often quoted and referenced that "if no manuscripts of the New Testament were extant, the New Testament could be reproduced from the writings of the early Fathers alone."[25]

Modern Sources

For the modern scholar, there are mainly two lines of evidence to discover the truthfulness of an ancient account. One is archaeological confirmation, and the other falls in the realm of the historian. Archaeology provides hard clues, perhaps inscriptions, buildings, or artifacts. The historian essentially matches up cultural, geographical, linguistic, and other anthropological aspects to gauge an accounts truthfulness regarding the time and culture it claims to be set in. These two disciplines are hopelessly intertwined in that they continuously borrow from one another to draw their conclusions. Additionally, when it comes to ancient texts they answer the same question, "Do the reports correspond to reality?"

It should be understood before going any further, that these disciplines are not the "be all end all" of ancient study, but they do provide strong corroboration. However, the further back in history one goes, the harder it becomes to verify the details. This is true in biblical study as well as any other area. Nevertheless, there is still sufficient reason to believe that the biblical writers gave truthful reports of actual events. Perhaps the best place to start is with Luke, since he claims to have conducted an investigation into the biblical accounts.

It has been noted, that much of the negative criticism associated with the Bible, and specifically the New Testament, are not based on archaeological and historical study, but rather, they are based on philosophical presppositions.[26] In this sense, it was exploited that any failure for archaeology to confirm a biblical account was noted as a contradiction. This, however, was not the case—and it is now not a common conclusion since the advancement of archaeological and historical studies only further corroborates the Bible with each passing year. Luke has fallen under this challenge many times. It is in fact true that he was at one point thought to be completely inaccurate. However, as archaeology progressed, it became apparent that Luke was so much more accurate than anyone could have hoped he was. "Luke manifests an array of knowledge of local places, names, conditions, customs, and circumstances that befit only an eyewitness contemporary of the time and events,"[27] and Geisler concludes of Luke's work, "Nothing like this amount of detailed confirmation exists for any other book from antiquity."[28]

The trend of philosophical presuppositions (i.e. naturalism, or atheism) being the prime basis for criticism against the Bible pushes back into the Old Testament as well. Foregoing the more "modern" Old Testament accounts (From king David and on into the prophetic writings—things which have ample archaeological confirmation) and going back to the further reaches to Abraham's time, it is noted that archaeology does nothing to prove Abraham's existence. Historically, however, there is nothing to discredit his existence either. So, while some may be inclined to point out that there is no archaeological verification, others might reply simply with the question, "Why would there be?" Apart from God's covenant, there is nothing inherently special about Abraham. By biblical accounts, he is a wanderer; and by historical accounts, he was a wanderer in a time and land of wanderers. In other words, for what is known of the times Abraham lived in (through historical study), even though there is no explicit verification for him personally (through archaeological study), the events described by the Bible, the cultures portrayed, the customs and other such types of descriptions found in the biblical accounts do match up to what should have been going on at the time. This is how the historian identifies fraudulent accounts because they simply do not match up, but the Old Testament time and time again lines up with what is known, even when archaeological evidence is scant. The statement, "Only presuppositions that rule out God's involvement with humankind can sustain the contention that these are merely legends devised to explain Israelite origins,"[29] rings true from end to end of the Old Testament.

Notice of Intent

There is ample reason to trust the biblical authors as truthful reporters of actual events. However, there is a meaningful caveat that needs to be attached to this truth. It should be understood that the writers are only reporting true and accurate events corresponding with historical reality insofar as they claim to be. This is not to say that the writer must declare, "I am telling the truth about actual events!" before each piece of literature that does just that. What it does mean is that not every piece of literature found in the Bible is intended to be read as that literal-type form of correspondence. Such things as poetry, proverbs, metaphors, hyperbole, parables, and other literary devices simply are not attempts to declare reality in a correspondence sense. While it is accurate to say these forms of literature are used to express truths, they should not be held to a rigid standard that would force them to be something other than what they actually are.

Nevertheless, from here on, it should be understood that the histories, prophecies, narratives, gospels, epistles, teachings, and all the other writings intended to be taken literally as historical records, do in fact record the truth. There simply is no justifiable reason to believe anything other than that the authors were truthfully reporting actual events. Any line of reason that contends against this declaration does so not from evidence of any sort, but from philosophical preconditions which prevent them from receiving the accounts as truthful—or, they simply do not like what the ancient authors reported and, therefore, reject the reports. But what is there not to like that would prompt so many, even so many of respectable scholarship, to go against scholarly protocol and reject a work without reasonable grounds to do so?

Establishing the Events Recorded in the Bible as God's Self-Revelation

Here lies the heart of the matter; here is what is not to like for some. If the Bible did not declare within its pages the non-negotiable self-revelation of God, then many would not have such a problem with its validity. On the other hand, if the Bible did not contain God's non-negotiable self-revelation, why would so many bother with it in the first place? So, having established that truth actually exists, and having good reason to believe that the authors of the writings contained in the Bible gave truthful accounts of actual events, it is here the place to establish that these truthful events are actually the records of God's self-revelation.

Dr. Norman Geisler asks the question, "If God has not unveiled Himself, then how can He be known?"[30] How indeed could he be known? Thankfully, Dr. Geisler answers his own question, "God has chosen to disclose Himself, and His self-disclosure is called revelation."[31] It is popular opinion in some circles that God is unknowable; other circles insist that there is no verification for God's existence. The Scriptures, however, offer responses to both these ideas, and the response is revelation—general, and special.

In the first chapter of Romans, Paul writes, "The wrath of God is being revealed from heaven against all the godlessness and wickedness of people, who suppress the truth by their wickedness, since what may be known about God is plain to them, because God made it plain to them (NIV)."[32] Notice that Paul speaks of knowable truth about God via his self-revelation, and the rebellion of mankind against this truth via suppression. What Paul goes on to say best describes general revelation, and it answers the circle of thought that insists there is no verification for God's existence, "For since the creation of the world God's invisible qualities—his eternal power and divine nature—have been clearly seen, being understood from what has been made, so that people are without excuse (NIV)."[33] With these verses, the Bible insists that there is no excuse to deny God's existence. Not only that, but it insists God intentionally revealed enough about himself via his creation for every person to be without excuse. According to these words, based off of what has been made by God, the cosmos (including the earth), one should be able to identify that God made it. If one maintains, as is somewhat popular today, that there is no evidence for God's existence, they directly contradict the truthful accounts of Scripture.

As noted, some do not feel general revelation goes far enough; they underestimate its potential to reveal God. There are others, however, who, as Ryrie notes, overestimate its potential to reveal God.[34] It should be expressed that, yes, a study of creation reveals its creator, but to know that creator, there would have to be more. This is where the other circle of thought comes in, saying that God is not knowable. And, this might be true if general revelation was all there is to the world, but it is not. Dr. Ryrie goes on to explain that general revelation is only volume one of God's great work.

The second volume, special revelation, is where God goes beyond revealing his existence to revealing his personality, his work in the world, and his will for humanity.[35] In fact, it is a strong position to assert that any true theology is only possible because God is willing and able to make himself known.[36] Oden says, "Revelation is not primarily the imparting of information but rather the self-giving and self-evidencing of God."[37] It is important, however, to understand what Oden is not saying. He is not saying one receives no information through revelation, but rather, that the main goal is not to gain new, arbitrary knowledge; revelation has a point.

"In the broadest possible sense," according to Roger Olson, revelation "is any way in which God communicates himself or something about himself to others."[38] Scripture, just like with general revelation, has something to say about special revelation. To any who would ask how God reveals himself, Hebrews answers, "In the past God spoke to our ancestors through the prophets at many times and in various ways, but in these last days he has spoken to us by his Son, whom he appointed heir of all things, and through whom also he made the universe. The Son is the radiance of God's glory and the exact representation of his being (NIV)."[39] What Hebrews is saying is that at one point, God did things a certain way, he revealed his will in a special way through prophets; now he reveals himself through is only begotten Son, Jesus Christ.

What the writers of the New Testament may not have realized, however, is that God was speaking through them, to his people of the future. This is the dual nature of divine revelation. In one sense, these men were simply trying to do their duties and record what they saw, others were trying to pass on what they were taught to teach others, while yet other times they were trying to handle situations under the context of what they received from the Lord; but God, at the same time, was having his book written exactly as he wanted it. Now, God has used many ways to reveal himself, dreams, visions, theophanies, angels, prophets, events, and finally,

Jesus Christ; the Bible, however, "serves as the most inclusive of all the avenues of special revelation, for it encompasses the record of many aspects of the other avenues."[40] This is what is meant by the Bible being God-breathed, or theopneustos, as Paul writes in his second letter to Timothy, verse 3:15, "All Scripture is God-breathed (NIV)." Perhaps Peter makes it even clearer when he writes, "Above all you must understand that no prophecy of Scripture came about by the prophet's own interpretation of things. For prophecy never had its origin in the human will, but prophets, though human, spoke from God as they were carried along by the Holy Spirit (NIV)."[41]

All of the data in this work leads up to one conclusion, that God has revealed himself to humanity in such a way that the men who partook in and witnessed his revelatory interactions made truthful and accurate records of it—which was always God's intention, to make himself known. The Bible is not arbitrary, accidental, or aimless; The Bible is God's self-revelation to mankind, and it is mankind's record of God's self-disclosure. Because of this, because of its very nature, there is ample reason to handle the accounts properly. In other words, if there is such a thing as truth—conditions which correspond to an ultimate and objective reality—then when dealing with that truth, it must be respected. Since the Bible is the truthful and accurate record of God's self-revelation to humanity, it is the only authoritative source for knowledge about him and his will for humanity; since the authoritative source for humans to partake in God's self-revelation takes the form of written records of actual events, dialogues, teachings, and situations, they must be translated, read, and taught from in such a way that presents the original message as it was intended by the original authors, or it does not reflect God's self-revelation and, therefore, does not carry the authority of God's word. The words may be no less than writings of men, but they are so much more; they are the direct communication from God, and, therefore, carry the full weight of his authority as if the skies opened up and his voice spoke directly.

Different Perspectives on Revelation and Scripture

It should come as no surprise that not everybody comes to the same conclusion about the Bible as has been presented here. The most obvious would clearly be naturalism/atheism. This view is not a primary concern of this work. Briefly, however, that view simply put, does not believe in anything metaphysical. Therefore, the Scriptures are nothing more than highly imaginative creations of men. Since there is no God, or since God does not intervene in the natural world, the Scriptures cannot be true records. The previous presentation has already addressed this view, and is why it will not be investigated further. What is to be discussed are views that handle the Scriptures in some sort of religious fashion, but with a different and erroneous approach.

LDS and Watchtower

The first opposing view is that Scripture is divine revelation, but it is not exclusive divine revelation. This view insists there is more to the narrative than what the Bible includes. As Olson notes, "Many sects and cults on the fringes of Christianity have produced or identified new revelations that stand in contrast to original revelation given by God in Jesus and through the prophets and apostles."[42] Two prime examples of this are the Watchtower Society of the Jehovah's Witnesses, and the Church of Jesus Christ of Latter-Day Saints. Both of these groups would openly identify as Christian, but both of them do not handle the Scripture in a right and proper way. The latter group, The Church of Jesus Christ of Latter-Day Saints, or Mormons for short, acknowledge the Bible, but only insofar as it is used and interpreted by their current leader (defined by them as The Prophet). They also have several other books that they hold to equal or greater authority as the Bible. In this sense, the Bible is not God's word, but rather a tool that can be used by their prophet to guide the Mormon people as he sees fit. The former group, the Jehovah's Witnesses, actually adheres to something closer to legitimate Christianity on the surface, but going deeper it becomes apparent that they do not hold to interpreting the Bible for what it says, which is equally as important as having the Bible in its proper place of authority.

In the case of the Mormons, the obvious problem is that the teachings coming from their extra-biblical books, and from their prophet, contradict the teachings in the Bible. Now, if the Bible truly is the accurate record of God's special, self-revelation regarding his will and his want for the redemption of humanity through his Son, Jesus Christ, then there should be no room for contradiction. If God is truly God, and truth is truly true, and the men who recorded God's truth in the Scriptures were truly accurate, then nothing can be added. And, as a point of note, if those things are not true of the Bible, then none of it matters anyways since there is no truth to what one can know about God.

In the case of the Jehovah's Witnesses, even though they claim to hold the Scripture to the highest authority, unlike the Mormons, they redefine key aspects of what the Scripture teaches in order to make it say whatever suits their established doctrine. In this sense, according to Dr. Walter Martin, they "use the terminology of the Bible and historical theology, but in an entirely different sense from that intended by the writers of Scripture."[43] The not as obvious problem here is that while the words remain the same, the meanings have been changed. In regards of objective reality, however, using the same words is irrelevant if they do not mean the same things as what was historically intended by God and by the original authors.

Both of these views have elevated further "prophecy" above that which was directly given by God, and should, therefore, be rejected. The Mormons do it explicitly by presenting extra works to be considered alongside the Bible, and honored above the Bible. The Jehovah's Witnesses do it in a backhanded sense by changing the meaning of the words contained within the Bible. Both of these views are in error, again, if the Bible contains historical truth. Whether one changes the words themselves or their meaning, one has departed from the truth.

Liberalism and Revelation

To go straight to the heart of the issue with liberal theology and revelation, it is that this school of thought does not believe the Bible is God's word. This is not to say they are atheists or unbelievers, but simply that they feel as if the Bible, while it contains snapshots of God's divine revelation, is not a complete, inspired, and infallible work of God. In other words, they believe the writers presented at times God's self-revelation, but they contend that one would have to sift through errors and contradictions to get to any of this revelation; they believe the Bible to be a book written solely by men about God. Geisler notes several flaws in this view starting with that it is inconsistent with the Bible's own claims to be the indestructible, authoritative, and "absolutely true Word of God."[44]

Also noted is that it is inconsistent for such liberal scholars to claim to be followers of Christ when, "A careful examination of the Gospels reveals that Jesus taught that the Bible is the divinely inspired and authoritative Word of God."[45]

In a fair assessment, however, there are positive contributions made by liberal theology such as a proper acknowledgement to man's part in the composition of Scripture, as well as a drive to pursue intense levels of scholarship to enable the study of the very Scriptures they do not view so sacred (another inconsistency pointed out by Geisler); however, "Whereas there are some positive features to the liberal approach to Scripture, such as the recognition of the Bible's humanness and the need for biblical scholarship, nonetheless, there are serious flaws in the liberal denial of the supernatural source, absolute authority, and complete historical reliability of the New Testament."[46] The issue, again, comes back to God revealing himself in a tangible, historical, and truthful manner, and his divinely ensuring that the Scriptures accurately reflect that revelation, and thus become that revelation. If this is not the case, then how can one know God?

Experiential Reckoning

This mindset may fall in with the liberal theology movement, but is somewhat different from the previous, academic liberalism in that it is more of an emotional liberalism. In this view, God is not revealed in an absolute and objective sense by the Scripture, but rather, he is revealed in our experience. Now, in truth, the Bible records mankind's experiences with God, and thus bear God's authority to be used as the curriculum to teach about him. This view is different, however. It denies "that we can know anything about God in himself," and it affirms that, "We can know God only in his effects on us, felt in our feelings; theology is the study of these effects."[47]

This view suffers greatly in its subjectivity. If this were the true view of reality about God and creation, then there would be no truth. The person who feels as if God blesses their extramarital affair would be just as right as the person who feels as if God desires one man and one woman to cleave together and become one flesh. This would make God a being of confusion, contradiction, and inconsistency. It would also go directly against the insistent truth that God wants his creation to know him, since he could never truly be known. Perhaps the most troubling points of this view is that it makes each individual the Lord of their own world, where their emotions are law, and no person or thing could challenge them. This theology says, "If it feels good do it, because good feelings come from God." To take it to its most fundamental flaw, though, this view cannot be the truth about God because it cannot correspond to reality in an objective sense—God is reduced to become the product of seven billion subjective sets of feeling about him, making him everything and nothing all at the same time. The only way for God to be known, as previously stated, is if he makes himself known—which he has done in the Bible. This is why a literal-historical view of Scripture is superior to any other for knowing God, his personality, and his will for mankind.

Conclusion

It is a sad state of affairs that the world has come so far off its hinges as to deny the very existence of reality, but denial or acknowledgement has no bearing on reality because by virtue of its fundamental nature, reality exists apart from any opinion or belief about it. This is how the world can be sure of the existence of truth, because it is that which corresponds to reality. In line with that objectivity, chosen men from chosen people recorded the truth about God as he revealed himself to humanity. It is only this truth that corresponds to reality. These oracles, these Scriptures, were given by God, coming from him and belonging to him, even though produced freely by men. They carry the full weight of God's authority as his self-disclosure. Therefore, the Bible and the lessons taught from it only retain their quality of God-breathed authority insofar as they are translated, read, and taught from in accordance with the original intended message that God inspired. Otherwise, if one does not present what the original authors were inspired to communicate, they present their own ideas, their own messages, and their own teachings which do not carry the weight and authority of God-breathed (theopneustos) Scripture.

Application

Since the Bible is a historical work, it is meant to be taken literally. That is to say, it is meant to be read as the original authors intended. To do this, one must approach the study of Scripture reverently and with a method, an applicable plan to reap consistent and accurate results. The Bible is both human records of divine revelation, and divinely inspired messages from God about who and what he is, and what he expects of us regarding our relationship with him. Because of this, the Bible is meant to be studied. Studied as the faithful words of God's people before us, and studied as the authoritative and inspired words of God himself. This means that the study must not be flippant or arbitrary, no Bible roulette, no mystical codes or secret teachings, and with no higher authority.

The tried, tested, and true means by which the serious student or seeker of God's truth can go about reading and studying the Bible is called by many the inductive study method. This seeks to accurately discover what the original author intended to say, and then apply it to the life of the reader today. This is done through observation, interpretation, and application. There are some variable additions, such as generalization and implementation, but these three are the core. For observation, one does just that—they observe. What does it say? In this phase, the student will read the passage, chapter, or book several times. They will note any distinctions in the text. They will note the author, they will note the audience, they will note historical setting, they will note how the current passage fits in with the previous and following section, and they will note any repeated phrases, questions asked, or literary devices. The student will note any and everything they can to help them truly know what the passage says.

Once considerable observation has taken place, the reader will then set about the task of interpretation, asking, "What does it mean?" This is highly important because the first thing a person wants to ask is, "What does this mean to me?" But that is not the right question. The proper question is what it means to the original author and to the original reader. What it means to a person in the 21st century with an Americanized worldview is virtually irrelevant to honest Bible study. Through continuity, context, and customary reading, one can arrive at the one and only proper interpretation of a passage, its original intended meaning.

The final stage in the process is application. After studying what the text says, and investigating what the text means, one can then, and only then, prayerfully consider how the text applies to them. It has been noted that there is a strong temptation to jump straight from observation to application, but this is a perilous mistake, "care must be taken to hear the Word of God as the original readers or hearers did and to find out what the Spirit of God was teaching them."[48] Because God interacted with mankind historically, in actual situations, there is a reality to the accounts recorded in the Bible. This means one can have a true understanding or a false understanding of them. This is why the process is so important, and it is ultimately why one arrives here naturally from the conclusion of the study of the doctrines of Revelation and of Scripture. If one arrives at a false conclusion of the meaning of a passage, and then tries to apply that false conclusion to their lives, then they are not going forth with God's authority—their applications do not correspond to reality because their interpretation does not correspond with reality. Therefore, let the reader investigate the truthful and accurate accounts of God's self-revelation with a method that honestly seeks to glean the reality of what took place, what it means, and how it applies to them.

APPENDIX 3

Introduction

This final appendix is a paper I wrote for Regent University's undergraduate course on Pauline literature. The point of including it here in my current work is because I think it accurately reflects on how one might go about studying through an entire work of the Bible. Here I seek to identify Paul's central theme in the book of Philippians, discuss how everything else in the letter is somehow related to this central theme, and then identify this theme throughout other pieces of the author's work in the New Testament. In a sense, I feel like this is exegetical and inductive Bible study 101. So, I hope this serves as a good example after everything we have discussed so far, and I pray that far beyond any conclusions I have come to within the work, that the process will be most what is gleaned from this final section.

Excursus on Humility: Tracing Paul's Argument for Humility Through his Letter to the Philippians

How doctrinal ideas on virtue and vice come about is an interesting concept compared to how other "hard" doctrines of orthodoxy and orthopraxis are established. While many of these more concrete doctrines of theology are defined and expressed in a systematic way, the belief and practice of virtuous ideals is often developed in a more thematic way. There are many examples within Scripture documenting the thematic presentation of various virtuous standards, mindsets, or lifestyles. This work will hone in on one particular epistle in the New Testament written by the apostle Paul. Here it will be shown how Paul's brilliant and beautiful Hellenistic styled rhetoric manages with elegant mastery to systematically unfold a thematic lesson—all while simultaneously addressing specific and personal issues to a group of believers perhaps holding a more intimate friendship with Paul than any other church in 1st century Christianity.

Various other pieces of the Pauline corpus are also surveyed for additional signs of the presently presented virtuous theme. In addition, the importance of this theme, its significance in biblical application for the Christian life, and its ultimate implementation in personal lives, church congregations, and general society is presented. Before any of that is discussed, however, the theme itself and its contextual medium of discussion must first be introduced.

Humility Throughout Philippians

The epistle to the church at Philippi is more than simply the pages on which the apostle Paul speaks of humility; similarly, humility is more than simply an occasional suggestion of Paul to the church at Philippi. This is pointed out to explain, in part, the difficulty of introducing one without the other (one being humility, and the other being Philippians). The two are dance partners of sorts. Where humility leads Philippians follows, and when Philippians leads humility follows.

Humility

Perhaps the biggest exegetical challenge to modern readers of ancient texts is leaving behind the modern world, with all its modern terms, phrases, and understandings, and traveling back to the ancient world in view. This, however, is a well-known necessity for the serious seeker of first-century understanding. Humility, then, as the main theme of this work, must be understood and examined in the same way. That is, humility must be examined, understood, and discussed as Paul meant it to be examined, understood, and discussed—not as we might know the concept in a contemporary sense.

It is, then, of a wonderful benefit to the modern world that Paul chose to define and illustrate his concept of humility within the context of the very medium which he presents it. This definition and illustration begins in the second chapter of Philippians. Paul writes, "Do nothing form selfish or empty conceit, but with humility of mind regard one another as more important than yourselves; do not merely look out for your own personal interests, but also for the interests of others (NASB)."[1] Following this definition, Paul provides an account of the self-emptying of Jesus Christ as an illustration. This is important because the humility Paul presents, the humility that he argues for throughout the entirety of his letter, is a virtue springing from the very character of God.[2]

This concept of Christ's humility, his self-emptying, is known in the scholarly community as the kenosis concept—a concept which many have devoted much time and effort to understanding. Regarding that, as renowned author and biblical scholar, Dr. Charles C. Ryrie puts it, "If our understanding of kenosis comes from Philippians 2, we should get our definition of the concept there."[3] This is, after all, the reason Paul includes the kenosis passage—to further define humility. In a biblical context, humility has a broader meaning than Paul intends here. In summation, humility is both used as, "A condition of low estate which will be brought about through the judgment of God,"[4] and also as, "A spirit of lowliness which enables God to bring the blessing of advancement."[5] Paul's use of humility in Philippians ultimately reflects the latter of the two meanings.

The most important thing to keep in consideration moving forward is that Paul's definition of humility and use of the kenosis passage are central to everything else in the epistle. Everything Paul says before chapter 2 is pointing toward kenosis, and everything Paul says afterward is looking back to kenosis.

The Epistle to the Philippians

"Philippians was one letter, written by the apostle Paul from Rome in the early 60's to his longtime friends and compatriots in the gospel."[6] The church at Philippi was the first one planted in Europe by Paul, and this letter to them, "Is the most personal of all his letters."[7] This intimate aspect is of utmost importance according to professor of New Testament studies, Dr. Gordon Fee, who claims many often overlook it while examining the rhetorical details of Paul's presentation[8] –not that the rhetorical devices are not present or important, but Paul's great love for his friends should be understood as the motivation for his rhetorical attempts to get their attention and inspire conviction in their hearts.[9]

Although Paul writes in thanks for the Philippians sending a monetary gift during his imprisonment in Rome (a distinction which is debated among scholars, but, "because of the weaknesses of arguments to the contrary, the traditional view that Paul writes

Philippians from Rome remains the best."[10]), he is also "concerned about their 'Christ-likeness,' which in this letter is clearly spelled out as 'God-likeness.'"[11] There is, apparently, an issue of pride and ill-regard for one another stifling the progress of the gospel. Paul would have received word of this through the messenger who brought the monetary gift, Epaphroditus. Paul's "major concern" for the Philippians, then, "Is that they get their corporate act together for the sake of the gospel."[12]

Paul calls the Philippians to imitate, "God's own character, 'humbleness of mind,' which is defined in terms of 'putting the needs of others before one's own,' and exemplified by the One who as 'equal with God' poured himself out into our humanity and in that humanity humbled himself to the ultimate obedience of death on a cross."[13] For numerous reasons, Paul goes through great lengths to argue his case for humility. One particularly important reason being that humility was seen as a bad thing in the ancient Greco-Roman world.[14] It, therefore, makes sense for Paul to make such a persuasive and thorough argument for humility as a virtue. More importantly, however, is the issue of Euodia and Syntyche, the two beloved pillars in the Philippian church causing division through their personal dispute. Paul wants to correct them, but he wants to do so lovingly. Understanding Philippians in this context helps one see why Paul lays out such a complete and vivid argument for humility, using the most extreme example of Jesus Christ, before finally calling his two beloved friends to examine their own behavior in light of everything previously said.

Analysis

Even though Philippians is an intimate epistle, written to a group of close friends, yokefellow as it were, Paul has a point to make—a lesson he wants to teach his friends. Considering that, it is no surprise to pick up on numerous stylistic distinctions. From one point of view, for instance, Philippians loosely follows the basic ancient format for a friendly letter.[15] From another point of view, paradigmatic themes and motifs, and structured argumentative rhetoric is easily detected.[16] It is important, as pointed out by Fee previously, to keep both aspects in view—particularly because both aspects meet and intertwine at the climax of the letter/argument in chapter 4.

From whichever vantage one chooses to examine Philippians, it can hardly be overlooked that the majority of onlookers and exegetes agree with the centrality of the Christological presentation in chapter 2. For this reason, despite briefly gazing upon it in the introduction, a closer look at chapter 2 will be the foundation from which this analysis is constructed.

The Christological Foundation

Have this attitude in yourself which was also in Christ Jesus, who, although He existed in the form of God, did not regard equality with God a thing to be grasped, but emptied Himself, taking the form of a bondservant, and being made in the likeness of men. Being found in appearance as a man, He humbled Himself by becoming obedient to the point of death, even death on a cross. For this reason also, God highly exalted Him, and bestowed on Him the name which is above every name, so that at the name of Jesus every knee will bow, of those who are in heaven and on earth and under the earth, and that every tongue will confess that Jesus Christ is Lord, to the glory of God the Father (NASB).[17]

This short passage, according to Ryrie, spawned many false ideas and understandings of Christology.[18] When viewed in the proper context, however, it seems difficult to arrive at a false conclusion. It is, then, of utter importance to ask oneself, "Why is Paul saying this?" What is the proper context? It is just that, context. One must view the passage precisely in light of the circumstance in which it is presented. When this is the case, it becomes easy to see "Paul's primary concern is not theological as such, but illustrative."[19] In fact, many view this passage as an ancient hymn that Paul included as a point of reference to invoke an explicit understanding in the minds of his audience as he makes his point. In any event, "Whether or not a hymn," according to professor emeritus of New Testament and Greek, Dr. Robert Gundry, "the passage is incidental to an exhortation to church unity through humility, of which humility Jesus provides the great example."[20] This point is agreed on even by ones who think Paul himself wrote this narrative of Christ, such as New Testament scholar N.T. Wright, who says, "I still hold the view that Paul wrote the poem himself, quite possibly for use at this point in this letter, and he certainly used it here in a way that integrates closely with the thrust of the letter as a whole."[21] In Short, then, "A paradigm of 'selflessness' and 'humility' is the reason for the narrative."[22]

That Paul wants the Philippians to imitate Christ's humble example is really the thesis of his whole argument. This is the reason for the current re-examination of the passage. It must be firmly established that Christ's prime role here is "as the one who in his saving death fully revealed God's character and is thus the ultimate paradigm of life in the present."[23] This is more or less what Ryrie means when saying, "The full reality of Him [Jesus] being a servant is the point of the passage."[24] This might sound too simple of a concept except that Paul is trying to reach out to real people, and it should be no surprise that real people tend to be hopelessly selfish and self-serving. This is where the depth of what Ryrie, and more importantly Paul, is trying to say—specifically that, "Whatever the emptying [humbling of Christ] involved, it was self-imposed. No one forced Christ to come into this world and eventually die on a cross as our sin-bearer."[25] Paul wants his friends to willingly pour themselves out for the cause of Christ just like Christ willingly poured himself out to meet their need for a savior. He, therefore, lays out his presentation in such a way that prompts his readers to make the decision to humble themselves on their own. Again, every dynamic of Paul's argument ties into the example of Christ in Philippians 2:5-11.

Paul's Opening

Many times, a reader can inadvertently gloss over important details of a text because they are unaware of a norm or standard surrounding a particular literary device, or even because they are unfamiliar with the habits or tendencies of a certain author. A perfect example being that, "In contrast to most extant letters from the Greco-Roman world, Paul's 'introductory matters' are quite long, made so usually because they are full of items that foreshadow the concerns of the letter."[26] Even a casual look at

Paul's work shows this to be true; in regard to the current issue of his argument for Christ-centered humility, it is true from the very first words of Philippians. Furthermore, as it proves to be consistent of Paul to offer condensed bits in the beginning of a letter for later unpacking, it can safely be assumed that Paul already knows exactly what he wants to say in the body. Nothing, then, is haphazard. This applies specifically to Philippians, as critics find out when they try to say it is actually a collection of multiple writings instead of a single work. Upon examination, one finds that, "It is difficult to isolate one part of the letter from another because the same terms, word-roots and motifs pervade all of its so-called parts. Furthermore," and of particular interest to this survey, "the development of Paul's argument in one part of the letter often depends on what he has said in another part."[27]

Bondservant

It is, therefore, of significant importance that Paul chooses to identify as a "bondservant" of the Lord. Notwithstanding the fact that bondservant is not a word widely understood in the modern world, Paul is, in reality, using the Greek word "douloi" (slave)—and very intentionally at that. This is one instance of translation playing an important role to understanding, as Fee points out, "While 'servant,' found in most English translations, is an acceptable rendering, it also causes the English reader to lose something of its force."[28] He then goes on to explain how, "Douloi were so common in Greco-Roman society that no one would have thought it to refer other than to those owned by, and subservient to the master of a household...Thus, whatever else, the word carries connotations of humility and servitude."[29]

The fact that many do not have access to in depth explanations of biblical languages and cultures is, of course, a considerable setback to Bible study. Even so, consumer level tools are available, such as the Vine's Concise Dictionary of the Bible, which explains that when Paul calls himself a bondservant of Jesus Christ, the claim is, "That, having been bought by Christ, he was now a willing slave, bound to his new master."[30] All of this pours into the foundation Paul is laying to his argument for willing humility, which he, again, works at from the very first line of his letter by identifying as a bondservant of Jesus Christ. "He uses this language to designate any and all of those who 'serve' God as 'free bondslaves,' that is, as those who are free in Christ Jesus, but who have used that freedom to 'perform the duties of a slave' in the service of God."[31]

It should here be pointed out also, that this is not an arbitrary concept. It actually stems directly from God himself who gives it to Moses to present to the Israelites in Exodus 21, "If the slave plainly says, 'I love my master...I will not go out as a free man,' then his master shall bring him to God...and he shall serve him permanently (NASB)."[32] Of course, while it is easy for one in possession of a Bible to make this connection, it might not have been so clear to the Philippians. This is not necessarily problematic since Paul has a much more obvious goal with his use of the word 'bondservant' (douloi). "Of special significance in our letter," according to Fee, "is Paul's use of this word [douloi] in 2:7 to designate Christ in the humiliation of his incarnation."[33] The ultimate implication being that, "As God's ultimate suffering servant he humbled himself to death on a cross—on the Philippians behalf—which serves as the proper ground for the humility to which Paul calls them in 2:4."[34] This humility is, again, "the absolutely predominant motif in this letter,"[35] and the basis for Paul saying, "They are to 'have this mindset that is also that of Christ Jesus…A concern probably anticipated by this self-designation."[36] For the sake of Paul's argument, then, it is important to understand that even though he hasn't revealed it yet, he is undeniably identifying himself with the humility of Christ he is about to present.

Love, Knowledge, Discernment, and Righteousness

Moving down toward the end of Paul's opening greeting to his friends at Philippi, he prays for them in ways included specifically to enable understanding of the Christ-like humility he intends on presenting. While this might not be perfectly clear at the present moment in the letter, the things said now begin to make more sense as his argument unfolds. Also, other things may have been clearer to those in the ancient culture. For instance, in 1:9, Paul prays that their love will abound. What we in the modern age might miss, is, "As used by Paul, and following the lead of the Septuagint, 'love' first of all points to the character of God, and to God's actions toward his people based on that character."[37] This is, of course, important because it is that very character of God, in Jesus Christ, that Paul soon uses as the crux of his argument for humility.

As Paul approaches the qualifying agents in the first stage of his argument, he also prays the Philippians will have "real knowledge and all discernment (NASB)."[38] This thought is not left open ended; Paul wants the Philippians to known exactly why he prays, saying in 1:10, "So that you may approve the things that are excellent, in order to be sincere and blameless until the day of Christ (NASB)." The fact that Paul wants them to have real knowledge and discernment implies that there is some sort of fake or false knowledge and discernment that he wants them to avoid. According to philosophy experts Moreland and Craig, "Ever since the time of Plato, philosophers have tried to offer an adequate definition of propositional knowledge."[39] This means that epistemology, at least in some form, was an issue in the first century—probably even more so in a Roman colony such as Philippi than in, say, Jerusalem. Epistemology, loosely defined as the study of knowledge or what it means to 'know,' deals directly in, "Issues involved with an individual as an experiencing, believing and knowing first-person subject."[40] This begins to make more sense in light of the understanding that Paul wants his friends to have this real knowledge and discernment, "So that their faculty for making proper assessments about what is absolutely essential regarding life in Christ will increase."[41]

Far from an arbitrary or abstract issue in Paul's argument, an un-humble mindset regarding the personal trials of life would lead to a self-centered interpretation of situations and, thus, a failure to see tough situations as 'excellent' things of God. "An increased knowledge of God," then, "is what is needed in order for them to 'walk worthy of the gospel' and in the one Spirit contend for the gospel as one person,"[42] as Paul will call them to do in 1:27. Before one can get there, however, they need love, knowledge, discernment, and the 'fruit of righteousness,' which, as Paul is about to make clear, "Means to go the way of the cross, self-emptying so as to become servant of all in place of 'selfish ambition,' and in that servanthood, humbling oneself."[43]

Personal Circumstances

As stated previously, every significant thing said by Paul in Philippians somehow ties into his definition and illustration of humility in Jesus Christ—which is why this study began with an introduction of that illustration before tracking back to the beginning to see how Paul then builds up to that one main focus. The remainder of chapter 1 does this by connecting his statements on understanding the excellent things of God with his coming statements about the definition of humility—caring for the needs of others more than the needs of oneself. In one sense, Paul stating his personal circumstances is commonplace in an ancient letter;[44] in another sense, it serves to further the paradigmatic foundation of humility Paul is laying.[45] This humility of mind enables Paul to see the excellent thing of God coming from his imprisonment—namely that particularly unreachable people, such as the praetorian guard or Caesar's household, are hearing the gospel of Christ.[46] As one professor of biblical theology puts it regarding Paul's trial, "He understands the propaganda value of his situation."[47]

Not all is wonderful, however, as Paul points out by naming some of the difficulties coming along with his imprisonment. One such difficulty being that "some, to be sure, are preaching Christ even from envy and strife…thinking to cause me [Paul] distress in my imprisonment (NASB)."[48] This is where the real knowledge and discernment to see the excellent things of God comes into play. Paul says, humbly caring more about the salvation of unregenerated Gentiles than his discomfort, "What then? Only that in every way, whether in pretense or truth, Christ is proclaimed; and in this I rejoice (NASB)."[49]

Now, before moving on, it is important to understand it is not Paul's pain and discomfort that causes him joy—this is not what the Scripture is saying. "His joy is not over his imprisonment as such;" according to Fee, "that kind of morbid 'thanking God for all things' lies outside Paul's own theological perspective."[50] His pain is still real, his discomfort is still present, but his primary interest is not his personal situation; it is the best interest of those around him—their need to hear the gospel of Jesus. Paul is modeling what he will soon say in 2:3-4, "With humility of mind regard one another as more important than yourselves; do not merely look out for your own personal interests, but also for the interests of others (NASB)." Paul makes this mindset explicitly clear in verse 24 when he explains that while it would be better for him to go home to the Lord, it is better for them that he stays on in ministry.

The Fulcrum

Paul now approaches the pivotal point in his argument, the contextual definition of humility and illustrative example of Jesus Christ. Having been discussed multiple times in the preceding pages, the kenosis passage will not receive a thorough dissection here. There is, however, much that could still be said on both the passage itself and Paul's use of it. One should also consider the transitional verses between Paul's personal circumstances and his presentation of the Christ narrative.

"Conduct yourselves in a manner worthy of the gospel of Christ," Paul says, wanting the Philippians to be, "standing firm in one spirit, with one mind striving together for the faith of the gospel (NASB)."[51] One could reasonably conclude Paul is addressing an opposite circumstance here. In other words, there is a division of spirit among the community, a separated mind leading to conduct unbecoming for representatives of Christ. A considerable confirmation of this is given in chapter 4, but Paul begins to broadly address the issue here. This is, then, both a transitionary statement from Paul's personal circumstances, and a qualifying circumstance for the Christ narrative to come. That being the case, it is important for Paul to properly set the stage because, "The 'story' of Christ serves as a paradigm for the 'mindset' necessary for unity among them with regard to the gospel."[52]

Some have gone as far as to think the Philippian church was even splitting into factions fueled by personal ambition. While that seems a bit much to conclude from the text alone, it certainly leads to the relevant conclusion that, "The one way to prevent factions is to be lowly in mind and to esteem the brother better than yourself."[53] This makes sense because it is precisely what Paul calls his friends to do in 2:3-4. Regardless of the validity of the faction interpretation, it is clear that Paul addresses an issue of division of some sort, and he uses Jesus Christ as the comparative example or model for a proper attitude. One would be hard pressed to advance the idea of humility not being the main virtue promoted from the Christ narrative, and because it is well known that humility was seen as an undesirable weakness in the ancient world, Paul's promotion of humility as a quality of God-likeness to be emulated advocates a new understanding of humility. Or, as Wright puts it, "The poem suggests, above all, a radical redefinition of power."[54]

The Christ narrative, whether a poem or hymn, whether written by Paul or not, whether previously well known by the readers or not, is Paul's way of saying, "However it is you are behaving currently, if it does not match up with the mindset, attitude, and actions of Christ...then it needs to change."

First Call to Action

Following the kenosis passage is the first of three calls to action. Paul never intends his teaching to simply be the subject of intellectual musing, but rather, he intends to inspire change. Of course, change in behavior begins with a change of the heart and mind, but it is, nevertheless, that ultimate change in behavior Paul seeks—hence his calls to action. Paul says, "So then, my beloved, just as you have always obeyed, not as in my presence only, but now much more in my absence, work out your salvation with fear and trembling; for it is God who is at work in you, both to will and to work for His good pleasure (NASB)."[55]

Of primary importance, one should understand that Paul is not here saying to work for one's salvation with fear and trembling at the thought of going to hell. He begins the statement by saying, "So then," which is to say, "As a culmination of everything I just said." Reflecting on the reality of Jesus Christ, "Who as God did the antithesis of 'selfish ambition' by pouring himself out and becoming a servant, and as a man the antithesis of 'vain conceit,' by humbling himself unto death on a cross"[56]—death for the salvation of mankind. Being partakers in that eternally secure salvation, live out life with a serious consideration that, as a member of the body of Christ, God works through each person's every action. The previously presented humility of Christ, then, is implicit in Paul's call for the Philippians in 2:14 to, "Do all things without grumbling or disputing (NASB)," and so on through the passage as Paul makes his plea. In a similar vain to Paul's declaration in 4:13, the idea here is that one can do all things without grumbling or disputing through Christ who humbles.

A final note on Paul's first call to action. He closes this thought by saying in 2:17-18, "Even if I am being poured out as a drink offering upon the sacrifice and service of your faith, I rejoice and share my joy with you all. You too, I urge you, rejoice in the same way and share your joy with me (NASB)." It is perhaps easy to focus in on the drink offering aspect of what Paul says here—thinking of the Old Testament idea of drink offering and sacrifice. "There is," however, "nothing inherent in the imagery to demand this view; and there are significant grammatical and contextual reasons to doubt it."[57] It is, instead, the pouring out aspect of verse 17 that needs to be considered as the main focus of Paul's thought. This makes much more sense as it relates intimately with Paul's recent presentation of Christ pouring himself out in his incarnation and sacrifice. It is the self-emptying which Paul is calling attention to. This not only serves as the closing thought on Paul's call to action, but it is also the transitionary idea Paul leaves the Philippians with as he moves on to the next phase of his argument for humility.

Earthly Examples of Heavenly Humility

The next section spans from Philippians 2:19-3:14. Paul ended his first call to action with the idea of pouring oneself out, a notion drawn from the ultimate illustration of Christ's heavenly example of self-emptying humility. In this phase of Paul's presentation, he offers three earthly examples of people who pour themselves out for the sake Christ, for the sake of the gospel, and specifically for the sake of the Philippians. As noted previously, a key aspect of Christ-like humility is the willing self-emptying. Christ, "Deliberately set aside His divine prerogative and progressively humbled Himself;"[58] the point is, "He willingly emptied himself."[59] Paul's point, however, is to perhaps show this is possible for not only the Christ, but for the Christian as well.

Timothy and Epaphroditus

Paul begins with the example of Timothy, who was listed as a bondservant along with Paul in the opening verse of this letter. On top of whatever connotations that brings, Paul says in verse 20 that Timothy is of kindred spirit with him and seeks the welfare of the Philippians—with the implication being that he seeks it even above his own welfare. Paul attaches, in verse 21, that this is actually in the interest of Jesus Christ. Timothy's Christ-likeness is further implied when Paul likens him, in verse 22, to a son serving his father—a reference to Jesus Christ that can hardly be missed in this context. Furthermore, "What he says about Timothy," according to Fee, "sounds so much like his appeal to them in vv. 3-4, one must assume this to be intentional, and for their sakes."[60]

Paul's wording concerning Epaphroditus also seems intentional and equally as paradigmatic as all the previous narratives.[61] Epaphroditus is referred to as a "fellow soldier," in verse 25, implying someone who is ready to give their life in battle for the cause. This is reinforced in verse 27 when Paul states, "He was sick to the point of death (NASB)," and it is further made clear in vv. 29-30 when Paul tells them to, "Hold men like him in high regard; because he came close to death for the work of Christ (NASB)."

Understanding that Paul is actually seeking to accomplish multiple goals with his writing, such as a practical address to situations and circumstances involving the Philippians—including the fact that both Timothy and Epaphroditus are going to be sent to them—and a holistic presentation of his argument for Christ-like humility in the Christian community, enables one to see that Paul's comments on Timothy and Epaphroditus are "Written so as to present these two brothers as further models: Timothy as one whom they know to live for the sake of Christ, and thus for the concerns of others; Epaphroditus, as one who in his suffering for Christ that brought him near death did not flag in doing the 'work of Christ.'[62]

For Paul to Live is Christ

Paul's autobiographical passage from 3:4-14 serves the function of his final earthly example of Christ-like humility. Interestingly enough, while Paul, who never likes to draw attention to himself, lists himself last, his example matches most closely to the emptying of Christ he models. Perhaps this was Paul's intention. For Paul, bragging is extremely uncharacteristic, and yet he begins by saying in 3:4, "If anyone else has a mind to put confidence in the flesh, I far more (NASB)," before launching into his impressive pedigree and moral accomplishments. It soon becomes clear, however, that Paul has a point in his bragging, namely so he can boldly declare in verse 8, "I count all things to be loss in view of the surpassing value of knowing Christ Jesus my Lord (NASB)." Jesus Christ, of course, has an even more impressive pedigree and moral foundation as the pre-incarnate Word of God. "In the kenosis," however, "Christ emptied himself of retaining and exploiting His status in the Godhead and took on humanity in order to die."[63]

This humility of Christ is a major pillar in Paul's new Christian character. "While he cannot renounce—nor does he wish to— what was given to him by birth (circumcision, being a member of Israel's race, of the tribe of Benjamin, born of true Hebrew stock), he does renounce them as grounds for boasting, along with his achievements that expressed his zeal for the law."[64] Paul empties himself of his pre-Christian glories in order take on the humility of Christ. Not only that, but "The entrance of Christ into his life," according to Gundry, "caused Paul not merely to dismiss, but to renounce as liabilities, all his former assets as such a Jew."[65] The humility of Christ, the self-emptying, the doing nothing from selfish ambition, revolves around, as Paul says in 3:13-14, "Forgetting what lies behind and reaching forward to what lies ahead…the prize of the upward call of God in Christ Jesus (NASB)." Understanding that Paul is continuously building on the humility of Jesus Christ, "What he is therefore calling them to is to live in conformity to the gospel as that has been spelled out repeatedly in their hearing, and as it has been repeated in the Christ narrative in 2:6-11 and in his own that has just preceded."[66]

Second Call to Action

Following Paul's three earthly examples of the heavenly humility found in Christ, he gives what can be understood as a second call to action. Once again, the whole point here is not for Paul to provide "food for thought," as it were. He wants his friends to actually take action, apply these teachings to their own lives, and implement them with confidence and faith. Paul is straightforward and direct in 3:16-17. He says, "Let us keep living by that same standard to which we have attained. Brethren, join in following my example and observe those who walk according to the pattern you have in us (NASB)."

This standard Paul speaks of is the standard of Jesus Christ, which has been his main topic of discussion all along. His words here in verse 16 reflect back to what he just said in verse 12, "Not that I have already obtained it or have already become perfect, but I press on so that I may lay hold of that for which also I was laid hold of by Jesus Christ," and verse 13, "Forgetting what lies behind and reaching forward to what lies ahead (NASB)." This is all as it pertains to the humbling of the heart and mind; the standard of Christ is the standard of self-emptying. Not that any have obtained a full self-emptying in the here and now, but the standard already attained in the positional and heavenly realm is an emptying of oneself and a filling of Christ—hence the need to forget whatever earthly accomplishments are behind, and humbly look forward to the heavenly reality which is, in Christ, already attained.

Perhaps Paul is aware of the complexity in what he just said, because in verse 17 he presents it very simply, "Join in following my example." Once again, it is not that Paul is calling attention to himself for the sake of himself, but rather, "In every case, 'imitation' of Paul means 'as I imitate Christ.'"[67] Thus, Paul again ties into his meta-motif, imitation of Christ—which in the context of Philippians means imitation of his humility, his self-emptying for the salvation of mankind. Paul also mentions observing others who follow this pattern—likely a reference to the other examples given, Timothy and Epaphroditus. Paul's second call to action is thus both a call and a confirmation that he intentionally provided examples of Christ-like humility for emulation.

Climax: Euodia and Syntyche

As mentioned at the outset of this work, understanding the habits and tendencies of an author helps one to understand the significance of certain things that may otherwise be overlooked. The mention of Euodia and Syntyche is one such circumstance. "Paul rarely ever mentions anyone by name. But here he does, and not because Euodia and Syntyche are the 'bad ones' who need to be singled out; precisely the opposite, here are long-time friends and co-workers, leaders in the believing community in Philippi, who have fallen on some bad times in terms of their 'doing the gospel.'"[68]

It can reasonably be assumed that this "final appeal," "Is where much of the letter has been heading right along."[69] In other words, the whole case of humble self-emptying for the ultimate sake of the gospel has been laid out with Euodia and Syntyche in mind from the beginning. Because Christ-like humility is such a dynamic practice, Paul lays out an extremely dynamic case—the dynamics of which need to be understood and expressed by Euodia and Syntyche. Of utmost importance is their willingness; Paul does not *command* them to submit, he *urges* them to. It is not true and proper Christ-like humility if it is a forced action, so these two must willingly humble themselves. Secondly, Paul is not suggesting one submits to the other, but rather, he wants them both to empty themselves for the cause of Christ. The gospel work could not be accomplished without the incarnation. "There was no way [Jesus] could become a man and remain in the position He had in His preincarnate state."[70] Christ, therefore, poured himself out unto humanity. Similarly, there is no way Euodia and Syntyche can do their gospel work without pouring themselves out unto Christ.

Paul wants these two, and really everyone, to be as Jesus was. This is why, "Having 'the same mindset in the Lord' has been specifically spelled out in the preceding paradigmatic narratives, where Christ (2:6-11) has humbled himself by taking the 'form of a slave' and thus becoming obedient unto death on a cross.'"[71] Understanding this is easier said than done, Paul leads them through some encouraging instruction ending in 4:7, with the primary idea being that, "As they submit their situation to God in prayer, with thanksgiving, what they may expect from God is that his 'peace' will 'guard' their hearts and minds as they remain 'in Christ Jesus.'"[72]

Final Call to Action

Paul's final call to action comes with a final example of application. He says to the Philippians, in 4:9, "The things you have learned and received and heard and seen in me, practice these things and the God of peace will be with you (NASB)." This, of course, might perhaps seem like easier-said-than-done ramblings, so Paul, again, steps up and offers his personal experience in vv. 11-13, concluding with the iconic statement, "I can do all things through Him who strengthens me (NASB)." These are Paul's closing thoughts. Therefore, "Given the context, one should recognize this brief autobiographical moment also to serve in a paradigmatic way."[73] It is Paul's final example of application. "In the midst of their own present difficulties, here is what they too should learn of life in Christ, that being 'in him who enables' means to be 'content' whatever their circumstances."[74] This is, of course, only possible when one has emptied themselves of their own prerogatives, prides, and preferences in order to be filled with the humble mind of Christ.

Final Analysis

Paul's argument for humility is clearly seen from start to finish of his letter to the Philippians. He builds up, in the first chapter, to his main definition and illustration in chapter 2. From here he builds out with numerous supporting illustrations in the remainder of chapter 2 and throughout chapter 3. Finally, he brings his argument to its ultimate conclusion in chapter 4, revealing its purpose and practical application. Paul is a master of persuasive rhetoric, but, as pointed out previously, he is not arguing here simply for the sake of arguing. These are his friends, his beloved co-workers in Christ who care for him and support him in ministry, and he desperately wants to help them. Even so, Paul presents a thorough and complete argument for Christ-like humility to anyone who would honestly consider his words.

Humility in the Pauline Corpus

There are, perhaps, countless examples of Christ-like humility throughout Paul's writings. Understanding a reference may not necessarily use the specific word humility, opens the door for even more. Christ-likeness is undoubtedly central to Paul's practical theology, and humility is central to Christ-like living. This section will examine three examples of humility in Paul's other writings—Ephesians 4:1-3, Romans 12:15-16, and Colossians 3:12-13. To be of note, the view taken here is that all of the New Testament epistles bearing his name are in fact authored by Paul.

Ephesians

Ephesians being considered a circular letter intended for many "churches" makes Paul's presentation of humility all the more important. The terminology, phrasing, and central message of Ephesians 4:1-3 is so similar to Paul's message in Philippians that one cannot help but assume it is a central theme to his idea of orthopraxis. Paul writes, "Therefore I, the prisoner of the Lord, implore you to walk in a manner worthy of the calling with which you have been called, with all humility and gentleness, with patience, showing tolerance for one another in love, being diligent to preserve the unity of the Spirit in the bond of peace (NASB)."

In Philippians, Paul directly draws on his Christ narrative. Similarly, here in Ephesians, Paul is presenting his call to humility, unity, and worthy living directly following a Christ-centered passage in 3:14-21. Not only that, but by beginning his humility passage in Ephesians with the word "therefore," Paul is directly connecting it to what he just said in chapter 3 about Jesus Christ.

Romans

Romans offers a short and indirect reference to humility in 12:15-16. Paul writes, "Rejoice with those who rejoice, and weep with those who weep. Be of the same mind toward one another; do not be haughty in mind, but associate with the lowly. Do not be wise in your own estimation (NASB)." Even though Paul does not use the exact word humility here, he is essentially describing what he called the Philippians to do in chapter 2. Namely, being of the same mind in Christ, and considering others more important than oneself. When Paul says here in Romans to 'not be haughty in mind,' he calls them to exercise humility. Again, this is an indirect reference, but the core idea to Paul's Christ-like humility is present.

Colossians

Colossians offers a clearer, more direct call to Christ-like humility in 3:12-13, which reads, "So, as those who have been chosen of God, holy and beloved, put on a heart of compassion, kindness, humility, gentleness and patience; bearing with one another, and forgiving each other, whoever has a complaint against anyone, just as the Lord forgave you (NASB)." Even more specific than the Romans passage, or perhaps even the Ephesians passage, Paul follows his call to humility here in Colossians with a Christ-focused call closely resembling chapter 4 of Philippians. Colossians 3:14-15 says, "Beyond all these things put on love, which is the perfect bond of unity. Let the peace of Christ rule in your hearts, to which indeed you were called in one body (NASB)."

This passage, in relation to Philippians, has all the key elements of Christ-centered humility; unity in one body, love, the peace of Christ, and humility by name. These ideas and connections could all be examined in their own separate works to be sure, but the goal here is not to give each example an exhaustive treatment, nor is it to give Paul's corpus an exhaustive treatment. The goal is, rather, to show through a few examples that Christ-likeness, which Paul clearly spells out in Philippians as humble, submissive, self-emptying joining in the mind of Christ, as one body, for the work of the gospel, to care for the world's greatest need—salvation in Christ—even over one's own immediate needs and ambitions.

Conclusion

Paul's argument for humility in Philippians is important to Christians in the modern age for numerous reasons. It is a complete and in-depth definitions that includes an ultimate illustration and multiple practical examples. Of most importance, however, is the fact that Paul is not only providing Christians with an instruction manual for Christ-like humility, but he also provides a deep gaze into the character of God—a character of giving, of servanthood, and of self-emptying for the greatest good of others. When Christ set aside heaven to take on humanity, "His humanity subjected Him to trials and limitations,"[75] and yet he took on those trials and limitations despite any personal toll it may have taken on him.

In many ways, the modern Christian mentality is that of a consumerist mindset. Many go to church expecting to receive, to be fed, and to be filled. There is, of course, nothing wrong with wanting to be filled with the wonderful Spirit, blessing, and anointing of God. Paul's idea of true Christian living, however, is one of delayed gratification, in a sense. Just like how Jesus Christ was not exalted and given the name above all names until after he willingly poured himself out, so too are Christians in every place and in every age urged to pour themselves out for the sake of Christ—for the sake of the gospel. It is this willing self-emptying that makes room for one to be filled. What could the individual need more? What could the church body need more? What could society in general need more—aside from a saving knowledge of the Lord Jesus Christ—than an intimate acquaintance with, and a willing adoption of, the humble servant's mind of Jesus Christ?

NOTES

Chapter 1

1. Hanson, Robert A. 8 Steps to Spiritual Maturity (Xulon Press, 2004), 122.
2. Luke 15:10, *New American Standard Bible.*
3. Hebrews 13:5.
4. Hanson, 11.

Chapter 2

1. Ephesians 5:26.
2. Hillsong United. Hosanna. Hillsong (HIL), Hillsong Church T/A Hillsong Music Australia, 2010.
3. Ibid.
4. Psalm 118:26 and Zechariah 9:9 predict the coming king into Jerusalem. Although perhaps obscure to us, the authors of the original texts wouldn't have felt the need for any drawn out or detailed explanation of this since in their mind, most everyone knew what this meant; it was engrained in their culture.
5. All four Gospels present a tale of Jesus entering Jerusalem on a donkey. When the crowd shouted Hosanna, and blessed is he who comes in the name of the Lord, they were acknowledging Jesus as the prophesied king. Their cry of Hosanna was a plea for salvation. "Save us now, you are our king!" This is the meaning of Hosanna.
6. NIV Archaeological Study Bible: An Illustrated Walk Through Biblical History and Culture : New International Version. Grand Rapids, Mich: Zondervan, 2005.

7. Thompson, Frank Charles. The Thompson Chain-Reference Bible: The Old Testament and the New Testament : Thompson's Original and Complete System of Bible Study. Indianapolis, Ind: B.B. Kirkbride Bible Co, 1983.

8. Strong, James, John R. Kohlenberger, James A. Swanson, and James Strong. The Strongest Strong's Exhaustive Concordance of the Bible. Grand Rapids, Mich: Zondervan, 2001.

9. Vine, W. E., and W. E. Vine. Vine's Concise Dictionary of Bible Words. Nashville: T. Nelson Publishers, 1999.

10. Ferguson, Sinclair B., David F. Wright, and J. I. Packer. New Dictionary of Theology. Downers Grove, Ill: InterVarsity Press, 1988.

11. For a single volume, many prefer the Matthew Henry's Commentary, although the expositions can be somewhat dated.

For scholarly works, there are many options such as the Pillar New Testament Commentary, The NIV Application Commentary Series, and the New International Commentary on the New Testament.

When I am looking for a commentary, I search amazon for, as an example, Commentary on Romans, and I see what is in my price range and what the reviews say (Unless I know I trust the author, then I just buy it no matter what the reviews say).

Chapter 3

1. John 20:31.

2. Ryrie, Charles Caldwell. Ryrie Study Bible: New American Standard Bible (Chicago, Ill: Moody Publishers, 2012), 1223.

3. Blomberg, Craig L. Jesus and the Gospels: An Introduction and Survey (Nashville, Tenn: B & H Academic, 2009), 138.

4. Ibid., 131.

5. Ibid., 195-96.

6. Luke 1:1-4.

7. Luke 1:5-10.

8. Gaebelein, Frank E., J. D. Douglas, D. A. Carson, Walter W. Wessel, and Walter L. Liefeld. The Expositor's Bible Commentary With the

New International Version of the Holy Bible Volume 8 (Grand Rapids: Zondervan Pub. House, 1984), 826.

. McDowell, Josh. God Breathed: The Undeniable Power and Reliability of Scripture (Uhrichsville, Ohio: Shiloh Run Press. 2015), 180.

. Metzger, Bruce M. The New Testament: Its Background, Growth, and Content (Nashville: Abingdon Press, 2003), 89-95.

. Blomberg, 427.

. Ibid., 426-27.

. Ibid., 428-29.

. Hill, Andrew E., and John H. Walton. A Survey of the Old Testament (Grand Rapids, Mich: Zondervan Pub. House, 2009), 87.

. 1 Peter 2:2.

. 1 Corinthians 3:2.

. Hebrews 5:13-14.

Chapter 4

1. Hutchinson, Robert J. Searching for Jesus: New Discoveries in the Quest for Jesus of Nazareth—and How They Confirm the Gospel Accounts (Nashville, Tn: Nelson Books. 2015), 84.

2. McDowell, 185-87.

3. Ibid., 148-49.

4. Strobel, Lee. The Case For The Real Jesus (Grand Rapids, Mich: Zondervan, 2007), 32.

5. Ibid., 35.

6. Ibid., 81.

7. Blomberg, Craig L. The Historical Reliability of the Gospels (Downers Grove, Ill: IVP Academic, 2007), 61.

8. Strobel, 88.

9. Ibid.

10. Wilkins, Michael J., and James Porter Moreland. Jesus Under Fire: Modern Scholarship Reinvents the Historical Jesus (Grand Rapids, Mich: Zondervan, 1995), 222.

Chapter 5

1. Joshua 1:7-8.
2. Mickelsen, A. Berkeley. Understanding Scripture: How to Read and Study the Bible (Peabody: Hendrickson Publishers, 2002), 2.
3. Richards, Larry, and Gary J. Bredfeldt. Creative Bible Teaching (Chicago: Moody Press, 1998), 41.
4. Mickelsen, 23.
5. Geisler, Norman L. Systematic Theology: In One Volume (Minneapolis, Minn: Bethany House, 2011), 188-89.
6. Ibid., 188.
7. Mickelsen, 7.
8. Richards and Bredfeldt, 39.
9. Geisler, 169.
10. Ibid., 170.
11. Ibid., 172.
12. Ibid.
13. Richards and Bredfeldt, 39.
14. Ibid., 41.
15. Mickelsen, 15.
16. Geisler, 174.
17. Ibid, 175.
18. Ibid.
19. Ibid., 177.
20. Richards and Bredfeldt, 39.
21. Geisler, 177.
22. Ibid., 190
23. Richards and Bredfeldt, 39.
24. Geisler, 191.
25. Ibid., 190.
26. Richards and Bredfeldt, 41.
27. Geisler, 174.
28. Ibid., 175.
29. Ibid.
30. Ibid., 176.
31. Ibid., 187.
32. Ibid., 178.

Chapter 6

1. Fee, Gordon D., and Douglas K. Stuart. How to Read the Bible for All Its Worth (Grand Rapids, Mich: Zondervan, 2014), 43.

2. Ibid.

3. Ibid., 44.

4. White, James R. The King James Only Controversy: Can You Trust the Modern Translations? (Bloomington, Minn: Bethany House, 2009), 47.

5. Fuhr, Richard Alan, and Andreas J. Köstenberger. Inductive Bible Study: Observation, Interpretation, and Application Through the Lenses of History, Literature, and Theology (Nashville, TN: B&H Academic, 2016), 60.

6. Fee and Stuart, 44.

7. Fuhr and Kostenberger, 48.

8. White, 50.

9. Fee and Stuart, 46.

10. Ibid., 44.

11. Fuhr and Kostenberger, 61.

12. Ibid., 60.

13. Ibid.

14. Fee and Stuart, 46.

15. Fuhr and Kostenberger, 47.

16. Yamauchi, E. M. "Hellenism," in Dictionary of Paul and his Letters, ed. Hawthorne, G. F., Martin, R. P., & Reid, D. G (Downers Grove, Il: InterVarsity Press, 1993), 384.

17. Fuhr and Kostenberger, 47.

18. Yamauchi, 386.

19. White, 32.

20. Ibid., 33.

21. Metzger, Bruce M. The Bible in Translation: Ancient and English Versions (Grand Rapids, Mich: Baker Academic, 2001), 35.

22. White, 33-34.

23. Metzger, 35.

24. White, 35.

25. Metzger, 31-32.

26. Ibid., 55-64.

27. Ibid., 66.
28. Ibid., 79.
29. White, 40.
30. Fee and Stuart, 43.
31. Fuhr and Kostenberger, 67.
32. Fee and Stuart, 43.
33. Fuhr and Kostenberger, 47.
34. Romans 10:14-15.
35. White, 28-29.
36. Fee and Stuart, 37.
37. Fuhr and Kostenberger.
38. Fee and Stuart, 36.
39. Fuhr and Kostenberger, 48.
40. Fee and Stuart, 37.
41. White, 47.
42. Ibid., 48-49.

Chapter 7

1. John 4:15.
2. John 4:11.
3. Fee and Stuart, 28-29.
4. Fuhr and Kostenberger, 35.
5. Richards and Bredfeldt, 63-73.
6. Fee and Stuart, 21-22.
7. Richards and Bredfeldt, 65-66.
8. Ibid., 66.
9. Ibid., 67.
10. Ibid.
11. Ibid., 68.
12. Ibid., 69.
13. Ibid.
14. Ibid.
15. Ibid., 71.
16. Ibid.

17. Ibid., 72.
18. James 1:22, *King James Version.*
19. James 1:19-21, *New Living Translation.*
20. James 1:21-22, NLT.
21. Richards and Bredfeldt, 72.
22. Ibid., 73.

Appendix 1

1. D.R. Groothuis. Truth Decay: Defending Christianity against the Challenges of Postmodernism (Downers Grove, Ill: InterVarsity Press, 2000), 112.
2. Ibid.
3. Groothuis, 123.
4. S.B. Ferguson, D.F. Wright, and J.I. Packer. New Dictionary of Theology (Downers Grove, Ill: InterVarsity Press, 1988), 384.
5. Ibid., 384-85.
6. Ferguson, Wright, & Packer, 386.
7. J. Bingham. Pocket History of the Church (Downers Grove, Ill: InterVarsity Press, 2002), 149.
8. Ibid., 150.
9. Ibid.
10. Ibid., 151.
11. H.T. Kerr. Readings in Christian Thought (Nashville: Abingdon Press, 1990), 215.
12. T.A. Lane. A Concise History of Christian Thought (Grand Rapids, Mich: Baker Academic, 2006), 239.
13. Kerr, 223.
14. Ibid., 242.
15. Lane, 246.
16. Ibid., 252.
17. N.L. Geisler. Systematic Theology: In One Volume (Minneapolis, Minn: Bethany House, 2011), 270.
18. Ibid., 271.
19. Ibid.

20. Ibid.

21. Ibid., 272.

22. Geisler, 273.

23. Ferguson, Wright, & Packer, 387.

24. Lane, 273.

25. Ibid., 269.

26. Ibid., 271.

27. Ibid., 273.

28. Lane, 274.

29. Ibid., 274-75.

30. Ibid., 284.

31. Ibid., 291.

32. Kerr, 313.

33. Geisler, 285.

34. Ibid., 286.

35. Geisler, 286.

36. Ibid.

37. Ibid.

38. Ibid.

39. Ibid., 288.

40. Ibid.

41. Ibid.

42. Bingham, 162.

43. Ibid.

44. Lane, 253.

45. Ibid., 257.

46. Ibid.

47. Ibid., 257-58.

48. Ibid., 256.

49. Geisler, 325.

50. Lane, 258.

51. Groothuis, 112.

52. Geisler, 305.

53. Ibid., 326.

54. Bingham, 165.

55. Geisler, 313-14.

56. Lane, 257.

57. Kerr, 218.

58. Matthew 5:28, New American Standard Bible.

59. Geisler, 240.

Appendix 2

1. John 18:37, New American Standard Bible.

2. John 18:38.

3. Ryrie, Charles Caldwell. Ryrie Study Bible: New American Standard Bible (Chicago, Ill: Moody Publishers, 2012), 1333 (footnotes).

4. Groothuis, Douglas R. Truth Decay: Defending Christianity against the Challenges of Postmodernism (Downers Grove, Ill: InterVarsity Press, 2000), 62-63.

5. Ibid., 61.

6. Moreland, J. P., & Craig, W. L. Philosophical Foundations for a Christian Worldview (Downers Grove, Ill: InterVarsity Press, 2003), 73.

7. Ibid., 73-74.

8. Groothuis, 65.

9. Ibid., 67.

10. Ibid., 35.

11. Groothuis, 38.

12. Geisler, Norman L., and Paul D. Feinberg. Introduction to Philosophy: A Christian Perspective (Grand Rapids, Mich: Baker Book House, 1980), 87-89.

13. Ibid., 84.

14. Ibid., 94.

15. Ibid.

16. Groothuis, 41.

17. Groothuis, 12.

18. 1 Corinthians 15:3-8, New International Version.

19. Romans 9:1.

20. 2 Peter 1:12-16.

21. Luke 1:1-4.

22. Metzger, Bruce M. The New Testament: Its Background, Growth, and Content (Nashville: Abingdon Press, 2003), 93.

23. Metzger, 93.

24. Ibid., 95.

25. Geisler, Norman L., and William E. Nix. A General Introduction to the Bible (Chicago: Moody Press, 1986), 430.

26. Geisler, Norman L. Systematic Theology: In One Volume (Minneapolis, Minn: Bethany House, 2011), 346.

27. Ibid., 351.

28. Ibid., 353.

29. Hill, Andrew E., and John H. Walton. A Survey of the Old Testament (Grand Rapids, Mich: Zondervan Pub. House, 2009), 82.

30. Geisler, Norman L. Systematic Theology. Volume One, Introduction, Bible (Minneapolis, Minn: Bethany House, 2003), 64.

31. Ibid.

32. Romans 1:18-19.

33. Romans 1:20.

34. Ryrie, Charles Caldwell. Basic Theology: A Popular Systematic Guide to Understanding Biblical Truth (Chicago, Ill: Moody Press, 1999), 37.

35. Ryrie, 35.

36. Highfield, Ron. Great Is the Lord: Theology for the Praise of God (Grand Rapids, Mich: William B. Eerdmans Pub, 2008), 5.

37. Oden, Thomas C. Classic Christianity: A Systematic Theology (New York: HarperOne, 1992), 17.

38. Olson, Roger E. The Mosaic of Christian Belief: Twenty Centuries of Unity and Diversity (Downers Grove, IL: InterVarsity Press, 2016), 71.

39. Hebrews 1:1-3.

40. Ryrie, 71-73.

41. 2 Peter 1:20-21.

42. Olson, 78.

43. Martin, Walter, and Ravi K. Zacharias. The Kingdom of the Cults (Minneapolis, Minn: Bethany House Publishers, 2003), 27.

44. Geisler, 271.

45. Ibid.

46. Geisler, 273.

47. Highfield, 11.

48. Richards, Larry, and Gary J. Bredfeldt. Creative Bible Teaching (Chicago: Moody Press, 1998), 65-71.

Appendix 3

1. Philippians 2:3-4, New American Standard Bible.
2. Douglas, J. D. The New Bible Dictionary (Grand Rapids, Mich: Eerdmans, 1979), 547.
3. Ryrie, Charles Caldwell. Basic Theology: A Popular Systematic Guide to Understanding Biblical Truth (Chicago, Ill: Moody Press, 1999), 301.
4. The New Bible Dictionary (TNBD), 547.
5. Ibid.
6. Fee, Gordon D. Paul's Letter to the Philippians (Grand Rapids, Mich: W.B. Eerdmans Pub. Co, 1995), 1.
7. Hawthorne, G. F., In Martin, R. P., & In Reid, D. G. Dictionary of Paul and his letters (Downers Grove, Il: InterVarsity Press, 1993), 707.
8. Fee, 16.
9. Fee, 16.
10. Gundry, Robert H. A Survey of the New Testament (Grand Rapids, Mich: Zondervan, 2012), 470.
11. Fee, 52.
12. Ibid., 47.
13. Ibid., 52.
14. Gundry, 471.
15. Dictionary of Paul and his Letters (DPL), 551.
16. Fee, 50.
17. Philippians 2:5-11.
18. Ryrie, 299.
19. Fee, 198.
20. Gundry, 471.
21. Wright, N. T. Paul: In fresh perspective (Minneapolis, Mn: Fortress Press, 2005), 72.
22. Fee, 50.
23. Fee, 50.
24. Ryrie, 300.
25. Ibid.
26. Fee, 59.
27. DPL, 709.
28. Fee, 62.

29. Ibid., 63.

30. Strong, James, and W. E. Vine. Strong's Concise Concordance & Vine's Concise Dictionary of the Bible: Two Bible Reference Classics in One Handy Volume (Nashville, TN: Thomas Nelson Publishers, 1999), 38.

31. Fee, 63-64.

32. Exodus 21:5-6.

33. Fee, 64.

34. Ibid.

35. Fee, 64.

36. Ibid.

37. Ibid., 98.

38. Philippians 1:9.

39. Moreland, James Porter, and William Lane Craig. Philosophical Foundations for a Christian Worldview (Downers Grove, Ill: InterVarsity Press, 2003), 73.

40. Ibid., 72.

41. Fee, 101.

42. Ibid., 100.

43. Ibid., 104.

44. Fee, 106.

45. Ibid., 107.

46. Philippians 1:13.

47. Ellis, Peter F. Seven Pauline Letters (Collegeville, Minn: Liturgical Press, 1982), 119.

48. Philippians 1:15-17.

49. Philippians 1:18.

50. Fee, 124.

51. Philippians 1:27.

52. Fee, 156.

53. Weidenaar, John. 1965. "The mind of Christ." Reformed Journal 15, no. 6: 22-23. ATLA Religion Database with ATLASerials, EBSCOhost (accessed January 14, 2018).

54. Wright, N. T. Paul: A Biography (San Francisco, CA: HarperOne, 2018), 274.

55. Philippians 2:12-13.

56. Fee, 187.

57. Fee, 252.

58. TNBD, 547.
59. Ryrie, 300.
60. Fee, 265.
61. Ibid., 273.
62. Fee, 261.
63. Ryrie, 301.
64. Fee, 316.
65. Gundry, 473.
66. Fee, 361.
67. Fee, 364.
68. Fee, 389.
69. Ibid.
70. Ryrie, 301.
71. Fee, 392.
72. Ibid., 410.
73. Ibid., 435.
74. Ibid.
75. Ryrie, 300

Bibliography

Bingham, D. Jeffrey. *Pocket History of the Church*. Downers Grove, Ill: InterVarsity Press, 2002.

Blomberg, Craig L. *Jesus and the Gospels: An Introduction and Survey*. Nashville, Tenn: B & H Academic, 2009.

Blomberg, Craig L. *The Historical Reliability of the Gospels*. Downers Grove, Ill: IVP Academic, 2007.

Douglas, J. D. *The New Bible Dictionary*. Grand Rapids, Mich: Eerdmans, 1979.

Ellis, Peter F. *Seven Pauline Letters*. Collegeville, Minn: Liturgical Press, 1982.

Fee, Gordon D., and Douglas K. Stuart. *How to Read the Bible for All Its Worth*. Grand Rapids, Mich: Zondervan, 2014.

Fee, Gordon D. *Paul's Letter to the Philippians*. Grand Rapids, Mich: W.B. Eerdmans Pub. Co, 1995.

Ferguson, Sinclair B., David F. Wright, and J. I. Packer. *New Dictionary of Theology*. Downers Grove, Ill: InterVarsity Press, 1988.

Fuhr, Richard Alan, and Andreas J. Köstenberger. *Inductive Bible Study: Observation, Interpretation, and Application Through the Lenses of History, Literature, and Theology.* Nashville, TN: B&H Academic, 2016.

Gaebelein, Frank E., J. D. Douglas, D. A. Carson, Walter W. Wessel, and Walter L. Liefeld. *The Expositor's Bible Commentary With the New International Version of the Holy Bible Volume 8.* Grand Rapids: Zondervan Pub. House, 1984.

Geisler, Norman L., and Paul D. Feinberg. *Introduction to Philosophy: A Christian Perspective.* Grand Rapids, Mich: Baker Book House, 1980.

Geisler, Norman L., and William E. Nix. *A General Introduction to the Bible.* Chicago: Moody Press, 1986.

Geisler, Norman L. *Systematic Theology: In One Volume.* Minneapolis, Minn: Bethany House, 2011.

Geisler, Norman L. *Systematic Theology. Volume One, Introduction, Bible.* Minneapolis, Minn: Bethany House, 2003.

Groothuis, Douglas R. *Truth Decay: Defending Christianity against the Challenges of Postmodernism.* Downers Grove, Ill: InterVarsity Press, 2000.

Gundry, Robert H. *A Survey of the New Testament.* Grand Rapids, Mich: Zondervan, 2012.

Hanson, Robert A. *8 Steps to Spiritual Maturity.* Xulon Press, 2004.

Hawthorne, G. F., In Martin, R. P., & In Reid, D. G. *Dictionary of Paul and his letters.* Downers Grove, Il: InterVarsity Press, 1993.

Highfield, Ron. *Great Is the Lord: Theology for the Praise of God.* Grand Rapids, Mich: William B. Eerdmans Pub, 2008.

Hill, Andrew E., and John H. Walton. *A Survey of the Old Testament*. Grand Rapids, Mich: Zondervan Pub. House, 2009.

Hillsong United. Hosanna. Hillsong (HIL), Hillsong Church T/A Hillsong Music Australia, 2010.

Hutchinson, Robert J. *Searching for Jesus: New Discoveries in the Quest for Jesus of Nazareth-- and How They Confirm the Gospel Accounts*. Nashville, Tn: Nelson Books. 2015.

Kerr, Hugh T. *Readings in Christian Thought*. Nashville: Abingdon Press, 1990.

Lane, Tony. *A Concise History of Christian Thought*. Grand Rapids, Mich: Baker Academic, 2006.

Martin, Walter, and Ravi K. Zacharias. *The Kingdom of the Cults*. Minneapolis, Minn: Bethany House Publishers, 2003.

McDowell, Josh. *God Breathed: The Undeniable Power and Reliability of Scripture*. Uhrichsville, Ohio: Shiloh Run Press. 2015.

Metzger, Bruce M. *The Bible in Translation: Ancient and English Versions*. Grand Rapids, Mich: Baker Academic, 2001.

Metzger, Bruce M. *The New Testament: Its Background, Growth, and Content*. Nashville: Abingdon Press, 2003.

Mickelsen, A. Berkeley. *Understanding Scripture: How to Read and Study the Bible*. Peabody: Hendrickson Publishers, 2002.

Moreland, James Porter, and William Lane Craig. *Philosophical Foundations for a Christian Worldview*. Downers Grove, Ill: InterVarsity Press, 2003.

NIV Archaeological Study Bible: An Illustrated Walk Through Biblical History and Culture: New International Version. Grand Rapids, Mich: Zondervan, 2005.

Oden, Thomas C. *Classic Christianity: A Systematic Theology*. New York: HarperOne, 1992.

Olson, Roger E. *The Mosaic of Christian Belief: Twenty Centuries of Unity and Diversity*. Downers Grove, IL: InterVarsity Press, 2016.

Richards, Larry, and Gary J. Bredfeldt. *Creative Bible Teaching*. Chicago: Moody Press, 1998.

Ryrie, Charles Caldwell. *Basic Theology: A Popular Systematic Guide to Understanding Biblical Truth*. Chicago, Ill: Moody Press, 1999.

Ryrie, Charles Caldwell. *Ryrie Study Bible: New American Standard Bible*. Chicago, Ill: Moody Publishers, 2012.

Strobel, Lee. *The Case For The Real Jesus*. Grand Rapids, Mich: Zondervan, 2007.

Strong, James, and W. E. Vine. *Strong's Concise Concordance & Vine's Concise Dictionary of the Bible: Two Bible Reference Classics in One Handy Volume*. Nashville, TN: Thomas Nelson Publishers, 1999.

Strong, James, John R. Kohlenberger, James A. Swanson, and James Strong. *The Strongest Strong's Exhaustive Concordance of the Bible*. Grand Rapids, Mich: Zondervan, 2001.

Thompson, Frank Charles. *The Thompson Chain-Reference Bible: The Old Testament and the New Testament : Thompson's Original and Complete System of Bible Study*. Indianapolis, Ind: B.B. Kirkbride Bible Co, 1983.

Vine, W. E., and W. E. Vine. *Vine's Concise Dictionary of Bible Words*. Nashville: T. Nelson Publishers, 1999.

Weidenaar, John. 1965. "The mind of Christ." Reformed Journal 15, no. 6: 22-23. ATLA Religion Database with ATLASerials, EBSCOhost (accessed January 14, 2018).

White, James R. *The King James Only Controversy: Can You Trust the Modern Translations?* Bloomington, Minn: Bethany House, 2009.

Wilkins, Michael J., and James Porter Moreland. *Jesus Under Fire: Modern Scholarship Reinvents the Historical Jesus.* Grand Rapids, Mich: Zondervan, 1995.

Wright, N. T. *Paul: A Biography.* San Francisco, CA: HarperOne, 2018.

Wright, N. T. *Paul: In fresh perspective.* Minneapolis, Minn: Fortress Press, 2005.

Yamauchi, E. M. "Hellenism," in *Dictionary of Paul and his Letters*, ed. Hawthorne, G. F., In Martin, R. P., & In Reid, D. G. Downers Grove, Il: InterVarsity Press, 1993.